Non Fiction

Initial Thoughts on Education in the 21st Century: Pedagogies for Growth and Transformation

Rosa Parra

Copyright © 2025 Rosa Parra

Published by

All Rights Reserved. No part of this publication may be reproduced, distributed, or transmitted in any form or by any means—electronic, mechanical, photocopy, recording, or any other—except for brief quotations of the authors or editor.

Although the authors and editor have made every effort to ensure that the information in this book was correct at press time, the authors and editor do not assume and hereby disclaim any liability to any party for any loss, damage, or disruption caused by errors or omissions, whether such errors or omissions result from negligence, accident, or any other cause.

About the Author

Rosa Parra began her academic journey at the University of Granada, Spain, where she earned a Degree in Hispanic Philology, cultivating a deep passion for language, literature, and linguistics. Her drive to share this knowledge led her to the United Kingdom, where she completed a master's in education at Nottingham Trent University, solidifying her commitment to teaching and pedagogy.

Currently, Rosa is a lecturer in Spanish and Sociology at Nottingham College. Rosa's curiosity and passion for personal and professional growth have led her to explore the intersection of education and psychology. She is currently pursuing a second Master's in Jungian and Post-Jungian Studies at the University of Essex, integrating depth psychology into her work to enhance her teaching practice and support holistic learning experiences.

Table of Contents

About the Author 3

Introduction 9

Chapter 1: Strategies to Promote Inclusion in the Modern Foreign Languages (MFL) Secondary Classroom 11

    The Principles of Inclusive Education in MFL 14

    Strategies for Promoting Inclusion in MFL 16

    Inclusion, Equal Opportunities, and Legislative Context 19

Chapter 2: Mentoring and Coaching in Education 23

    Formal vs. Informal Mentoring 25

    Choosing the Right Model for Schools 26

    Key Features of a Hybrid Mentoring Approach 26

    Informal Mentoring: The Power of Authenticity 27

    Formal Mentoring: The Value of Structure 27

    Reimagining Mentoring for Modern Education 27

    Advantages and Disadvantages of Mentoring 28

    Maximising Mentoring Impact Through Clear Structures 29

    Emotional Intelligence in Mentoring Relationships 30

    The Risk of Mismatched Pairings 30

    Mentoring Styles and Functions 32

    Formal vs. Informal Mentoring: Advantages and Disadvantages 32

Chapter 3: Management in Teaching and Learning 35

    Leadership and Management of Teacher Assistants 39

    The Role of School Leaders 41

    Advantages and Disadvantages of Teacher Assistants 43

    Improving the Management of Teacher Assistants 44

Chapter 4: Innovations in Teaching and Learning 47
    Origins and Development of Wikis 50
    Advantages and Disadvantages of Wikis in MFL 51
    Addressing Key Issues in MFL Learning 53
    Catering to Different Learning Styles 53

Chapter 5: MFL Theory in the Secondary Sector 56
    Key Perspectives in SLA 58
    Practical Implications for MFL 59
    Implications for Learners 59
    Implications for teachers 62

Chapter 6: MFL and Leadership 64
    Goals and Objectives 64
    Leadership Influence the MFL Classroom 64
    Key Issues in Educational Leadership 66
    Diverse Performance 66
    Fairness and Equity: 67
    Celebrating Differences: 67
    Work-Life Integration: 68
    Positive Psychology in Leadership 68
    Leadership in MFL Departments 69
    Influence on the Classroom 69
    Leadership Styles Beneficial for MFL 69
    Practical Implications 71

Chapter 7: Reading a Foreign Language 73
    The Challenge of Developing Fluent Reading Skills 74
    Defining Reading Fluency 75
    Extensive Reading: A Path to Fluency 75
    The Components of Reading Fluency 76

Implications for Foreign Language Instruction 78

Chapter 8: Differentiation in Modern Education 83

The Principles of Differentiation 85

Compassion in Differentiation 86

Practical Strategies for Differentiation 87

The Impact of Differentiation 88

Chapter 9: Expertise in Teaching 90

The Nature of Teacher Expertise 90

Compassion and Expertise 91

Expertise vs. Perfectionism 93

The Impact of Expertise on the Classroom 93

Chapter 10: Teaching, Learning, and Leading Through Covid-19 96

The Challenges of Teaching During a Pandemic 96

Leadership During Covid-19 98

The Student Experience 98

Compassionate Teaching in Times of Crisis 99

Lessons Learned 99

Chapter 11: The Power of Mindset in Education 102

Understanding Fixed and Growth Mindsets 102

The Role of Mindset in Education 103

Leadership and the Growth Mindset 105

Practical Applications of the Growth Mindset 106

Mindset as a Foundation for Growth 106

Chapter 12: The Art of Listening in Education 108

The Importance of Listening 108

Leaders Listening to Teachers and Students 111

A Culture of Listening 111

The Practice of Compassionate Listening 111
The Impact of Listening 112
Conclusion: 112

Chapter 13: Braving the Wilderness in Education 115
The Wilderness of Authenticity 115
Relationship-Driven Education 116
The Role of Vulnerability in Leadership 117
Building Resilient Professional Relationships 117
The Wilderness as a Space for Growth 119

Chapter 14: The Role of Discipline in Education 120
The Discipline of Teaching and Learning 121
Compassionate Discipline 121
Developing Self-Discipline in Students 122
The Intersection of Discipline and Compassion 123
The Rewards of Discipline 124

Chapter 15: Love, Recovery, and the Measure of Education's Worth 126
The Measurable Value of Education 127
What Education Did for Me: A Personal Journey 127
The Role of Love in Education 128
The Necessity of Recovery 129
Repairing What is Broken 129
Balancing Love, Recovery, and Measurable Outcomes 130
The Legacy of Education 131

Chapter 16: Lifelong Learning and the Integration of Jungian Principles in Teacher Development 133
Jung's Vision: Education Beyond Formal Schooling 133
The Potential of Jungian Principles in CPD 134
Practical Challenges 135

Ethical Considerations 136
Proposed Directions for CPD: 138
Epilogue: The Lifelong Journey of Education 140

Introduction

Education is one of the most powerful tools we possess to shape individuals, communities, and societies. It is a dynamic, ever-evolving field that reflects the complexities of the modern world while simultaneously preparing individuals to navigate it. This book explores the multifaceted nature of education, offering insights and strategies for educators, leaders, and lifelong learners. Divided into two distinct sections, it delves into the specific challenges and opportunities of secondary education and Modern Foreign Languages (MFL) before broadening its focus to encompass universal themes in pedagogy and professional development.

The first section examines the critical role of secondary education, with a particular emphasis on the teaching and learning of Modern Foreign Languages. In an increasingly interconnected world, the ability to communicate across cultures is more important than ever. Chapters in this section explore strategies to foster inclusion in the MFL classroom, the importance of mentoring and coaching, and the role of leadership and innovation in the secondary sector. These chapters also highlight the theoretical underpinnings of MFL education and practical approaches to enhancing the experience of both teachers and students.

The second section transitions to broader themes in education and pedagogy, addressing the universal challenges and opportunities educators face. Topics such as differentiation, expertise in teaching, and the lessons learned from navigating the COVID-19 pandemic emphasize the resilience and adaptability required in modern educational contexts. This section also reflects on the emotional and philosophical dimensions of education, exploring the power of mindset, the art of listening, and the vital role of love, recovery, and discipline in creating meaningful learning environments. The final chapter introduces Carl Jung's theories on lifelong learning and their relevance to teacher development, offering a compelling vision for education as a continuous journey of growth and self-discovery.

This book is not just a guide for educators but also an invitation to reflect on the transformative power of education. Whether you are a teacher, leader, or lifelong learner, it encourages you to embrace both the measurable and intangible aspects of teaching and learning. From practical strategies to profound reflections, this book aims to inspire and equip readers to contribute meaningfully to the ever-changing world of education.

Chapter 1: Strategies to Promote Inclusion in the Modern Foreign Languages (MFL) Secondary Classroom

As the importance of inclusion in Modern Foreign Languages (MFL) education continues to grow in schools, so too does the recognition of the role MFL skills play in students' future development. This chapter aims to explore and analyse the most effective strategies for promoting inclusion in the MFL classroom, particularly at the Key Stage 3 (KS3) level. Effective inclusion strategies in MFL classrooms are those that ensure all students have equal access to learning and achievement, regardless of their diverse life experiences and educational needs. These strategies are essential for creating an environment where all students feel valued and capable of success.

As Cohen, Manion, and Morrison (2007, p. 283) argue, "An MFL teacher who puts in place strategies to develop inclusion will support students to understand that any barriers to learning can be addressed and overcome, will have their progress regularly monitored, and will have high expectations for all." The inclusion of all students in MFL not only improves their educational outcomes but also fosters a deeper appreciation for different cultures and languages, which is critical in today's globalized world. This chapter provides a review of key strategies proven to effectively promote inclusion in MFL classrooms and explores how they can be applied specifically to KS3 students.

When it comes to true inclusion, one doesn't look for the confident ones, it's about looking out for the students sitting at the back of the class, or perhaps the newbie joining us from an entirely different perspective – different culture, different language, and different world. We should also be on the lookout for those who are neurologically challenged – a learner with dyslexia who years for a different approach, slower pace, and time to adjust to the new entourage of words in their brain. This observation and recognition are the core of inclusion which is key in the MFL classroom. Here, language is the message and also the messenger, which makes it essential to help those students not only understand the curriculum, but also feel as if they are being seen by their teacher.

When practiced correctly, Inclusion feels less of a chore of a policy target and becomes a part of the mindset that radiates to all aspects of your teaching experience. It sprouts in the morning, as the teacher greets the students into their classroom, to the tiny tweaks made in the approach to the delivery of words to the dear listeners, and blossoms to grouping and setting up activities in a way that ensures that every child is included, is seen and heard. In an MFL setup, this can look like adjusting the speed to a slower more understandable cadence so that everyone in the classroom can flow in the same direction, or offering visual cards for those who learn with sight better, or making sure that instructions are given as such that every child, not just the clever ones, can understand and follow them to the completion of the task. These small adjustments that ensures that everyone is included, reflects the true meaning of empathy and professionalism in an educational setting.

Teachers who are working with Key Stage 3 students have a bundle of complexities to follow in their classroom. This can include cultural, linguistic, and or emotional diversity, which exudes the potential to improve, rather than outliers to accommodate; as students from different classes and creeds can be used as linguistical weapons. Let's take a pupil who speaks Persian for example: they might not be able to find grammatical similarities from German, but the crossover between those worlds could generate a beautiful harmony of improved classroom discussion. This is a great example of **amplification**; inviting more voices, more reasoning, and more knowledge to the classroom.

A noteworthy strategy to promote inclusion, that is criminally underrated, is including and mixing the students' home language into the curriculum. It can be as little as adding simple phrases from their native language around the classroom, to drawing parallels from the words and phrases in the syllabus to their language. Other creative ways, such as mini-presentations of their culture, customs, or traditions can heavily signal to those children that not only are they welcomed in the classroom, they are seen. It will show other students a slice of their home life to their peers, making them better at connecting with each other and the educator. This makes sure that interactions between students grow and they feel more at home.

Remember, inclusion in MFL teaching doesn't come off as an accident, it needs to be carefully woven into the very core of the education style of the educator. It is imperative that the teacher continues to be intentional with their inclusion, be flexible to learning, and continuously reflect on ways to improve their skills. The teacher needs to also dive deep into their old habits of teaching and see how they can improve. Some teachers are used to invite a few volunteers that are confident, or rely heavily on textbooks, that often lack the diversity needed for inclusion. This means taking accountability – admitting that old ways and mindset only drags back the crucial learning, and be willing to adapt to newer models of teaching.

Technology can be integrated into the classroom to build a powerhouse for inclusive MFL instructions. Adding tools such as online customizable flashcards, games that enhance language learning, or materials such as text-to-speech apps (for those who have difficulty reading, or need more auditory cues), and animated videos relevant to the topic can help cultivate an environment that invites students of all walks of life into the learning bubble. This helps provide them with additional support that enhances their learning experiences and connect better with the curriculum.

A key aspect to the inclusive MFL teaching is understanding the emotional sensitivity of language learning. Learning a new language – particularly one which you are not familiar with or resonate with – can be a daunting and mentally vulnerable experience. It can strike fear and anxiety amongst the new pupil who may be learning to adapt to not only just the new language, but also to the new environment. Recognising this vulnerability is imperative for an educator, as they can show support by celebrating small achievements, normalizing making mistakes, and provide a low-stakes environment, that offers opportunities to grow and learn. Teachers can use tools such as scaffolded sentence starters, anonymous response tools, or paired dialogues to provide a safety net to those who want to learn.

Another aspect of inclusion that needs to be added to the checklist is assessment. It has been noted that traditional assessment methods often boost those students that have a higher reading and/or writing skill; this ignores other aspects of learning which includes: listening comprehension, oral fluency, and creative expressions. By casting a wide net for assessment methods, we can gain a better picture of what the student is capable of, giving them a better chance to succeed. Teachers can modify assessments by adding elements of listening comprehension, oral fluency, and creative expressions by adding parts such as digital storytelling, oral interviews, peer feedback, and role plays. Remember, assessment is not just a means to put a score on a paper, it's about diversifying achievements to highlight the strength of every student.

Inclusion learning also includes collaborative learning structures into the curriculum. Peer interaction and group collaboration is an excellent way to introduce new point of views, diversifying knowledge, and build interpersonal skills. Group tasks, when done correctly, can not only bring a cumulation of different ideas and perspectives, but also encourage the enhancement of linguistics amongst one-and-other. Pairing can be done strategically – pairing the shy kid with the confident speaker allows the quitter voices to amplify, and create a sense of responsibility to uplift each other.

Amongst all, the top aspect of inclusive learning is the impact it has on the students' identity. Students who feel like they are being seen and understood are more confident. The support of the teacher fosters a sense of confidence, a willingness to improve and interact with others, and learn about other cultures other than their own. These changes are not just a tool to be used in the classroom, they are life skills for the students, making it not just a mode to understand better, it can also be a vehicle of empowerment.

Remember, inclusive learning is not just for the students to learn it is for the educator to learn as well. With each student comes a new chance to learn, grow, and challenge the structures and build new ways to enhance our craft. Inclusion is not a set list we can craft and follow rigidly, it's is a truly human experience, where things evolve as the days go by. MFL classroom provides a hub for improvement; to learn, to foster connections, where language and culture collide to create a harmony that helps improve lives.

The Principles of Inclusive Education in MFL

The Department for Education (2003, p. 8) laid out three guiding principles for planning and teaching in its statutory

"Framework for Teaching Modern Foreign Languages: Years 7, 8, and 9." These principles remain central to promoting inclusion in the MFL classroom: setting suitable learning challenges, ensuring that tasks are challenging but achievable for all students, responding to pupils' diverse learning needs and adapting teaching to accommodate different learning styles, abilities, and backgrounds.

In addition, Ofsted (2005, p. 9) offers an insightful definition of an inclusive school: "An educationally inclusive school is one in which teaching and learning achievements, attitude, and well-being of every young person matter. This shows not only in the performance but also in the ethos and willingness to offer new opportunities to pupils who may have experienced previous difficulties. This does not mean treating all pupils in the same way; rather, it involves taking account of pupils' life experiences and needs."

Recognizing that language is a combination of skill and an identity marker is key to creating an inclusive MFL classroom. It is important to note that everyone brings a unique blend of complexities with language. Some may be fluent in several languages orally, but find it difficult to duplicate that fluency in academic literacy. Others may be anxious to speak infront of their peers for various reasons. Here, inclusion means to recognize language as a tool to enhance learning, not as an obstacle. Those who honor the complexity of linguistics and integrate languages from other cultures to generate a curriculum that authentically supports students in these learning spaces.

Relational pedagogy is also an integral part of the MFL inclusion classroom. Relational pedagogy is a method that places trust, compassion, and understanding, in the hands of the students' voices while teaching. It is merely not enough to just change pace or make differentiated worksheets; a teacher needs to make sure that the children feel seen and heard. This could translate by highlighting their strong suites with activities such as: role playing, storytelling, collaborative projects, or creative expression through different mediums. All these examples help build confidence and brings every child to the platform.

Student Agency also plays a critical role in inclusion discussion which is often overlooked. Students, when given a choice, whether it is as small as picking grammar words, to themes that reflect their interest, are more proactive in the work, show more interests, and feel empowered. Students can engage better in peer-led activities, show various ways of understanding, and exude confidence in their work. This approach does not dilute learning or make it go astray from the path, rather it encourages readers and learners to engage in the material actively on their own accord.

It is imperative that a teacher in an MFL setting also incorporate the **hidden curriculum** in their classroom. This hidden curriculum highlights where one belongs, what knowledge counts, and what success can look like. This curriculum can be visible in the display material plastered around the classroom, the model language, and accents used in speaking sessions – all these emphasize the cultural atmosphere that the teacher has cultivated in their classroom and boost the feeling of belonging through the content being taught.

Finally, it is important to remember that inclusive teaching a whole-school commitment, not just the sole responsibility of the teacher. Teachers can create their personalized plans and inclusive strategies, but ultimately it is the responsibility of the leadership teams that have to provide an environment for inclusive learning. This can include policies that invites inclusion and diversity, CPD opportunities for the staff to learn more techniques and get better qualifications to enhance the inclusion experience.

These principles emphasize that inclusion is about more than simply providing equal opportunities—it is about actively addressing the unique needs of each student to ensure they can thrive. This chapter builds on these principles by outlining specific strategies that MFL teachers can implement to promote inclusion at KS3, the stage at which students are required to study a foreign language as part of the curriculum.

Strategies for Promoting Inclusion in MFL

The strategies presented here are designed to support inclusion in MFL classrooms and are particularly relevant for Year 7, 8, and 9 students. These approaches are based on research and statutory guidance, such as the Department for Education's 2002 recommendations and subsequent educational reports.

1. Lesson Design and Planning for Inclusion

Effective lesson planning is crucial to fostering an inclusive environment in MFL classrooms. The Department for Education (2002, p. 14) identified several key components of inclusive lesson design:

Starters: Begin each lesson by sharing the Learning Objective (LO) with the class. Use questioning techniques that are appropriately pitched to ensure every pupil can participate and encourage students to explain their thought processes.

Main Activities: Provide opportunities for students to work in pairs or groups to practice language skills. Offer targeted support tailored to individual needs and revisit the LO throughout the lesson to reinforce understanding.

Plenaries: Use the final part of the lesson to assess whether students have achieved the LO. This can be done through individual, pair, or group activities.

Extension Opportunities: Provide homework or other out-of-class activities that allow students to consolidate and apply their learning.

Pre-teaching key (vocabulary or structures) is often an overlooked, yet effective way to enhance inclusion learning. Before introducing a new topic, a set of material gets introduced to the learners that helps them digest the next topic better, equipping them with skills necessary to move further, and reducing cognitive overload. This can involve simplified texts for reading and writing, sharing audio and video clips, providing bilingual glossaries – giving students a chance to get the feel for the material coming ahead. This can be very helpful to build a solid foundation, making the children feel ready for the new material ahead of them.

Involving the five senses into the classroom can be a very effective way to boost learning in students. Using a **multi-sensory approach** can help engage the students more vividly in the new curriculum. Teachers can use various approaches, including but not limited to song, dance smells, visual cues, role play, and movements, digital tools for sound and visuals, or play to engage all the senses of the students. This technique can be very beneficial for not only those who are more of a visual or auditory learners, but also those who have neurological impairments such as ADHD, Dyslexia. Autism, or other learning difficulties.

Understanding the fact that inclusion learning is not reactive, it's proactive. This means that the teacher needs to map out and plan ahead of the lesson to support the learners rather than scrap up something in the moment. Planning ahead with lesson plans, worksheets, starters for speaking prompts for oral tasks, or crafting different pathways for writing activities can ensure that the children move towards a similar goal while learning at their own pace and accord. Inclusion is not just there to make things easy, it is there to ensure all children end up at the same destination after taking different paths; giving them a fair shot in life.

2. Building Positive Teacher-Pupil Relationships

Creating a supportive and inclusive classroom environment begins with the teacher. A strong teacher-pupil relationship can significantly impact students' confidence and engagement in learning. The following practices are particularly effective:

Encourage pupils to express their opinions and ideas without fear of judgment. Responding positively to incorrect or unconventional answers helps create a safe space for learning.

Demonstrate enthusiasm for the subject and maintain high expectations for all students while avoiding stereotypes and assumptions.

Foster a welcoming physical environment by decorating the classroom with colorful displays that highlight and celebrate pupils' work.

Small acts of conscious kindness have the greatest impact – pairing a meek student with a confident child to help them both share responsibility and amplify each other's voices, or remembering the native language of a pupil and giving nods to it by providing additional help such as bilingual glossary etc. can help a child feel at ease. It makes students more curious and involved. When someone feels left out, it is often noticed that withdraw from the group altogether. Making them feel seen and heard gives them a boost of confidence they need, increasing the joy of learning.

3. Assessment for Learning (AfL)

Assessment for Learning (AfL) plays a vital role in promoting inclusion by helping students understand what is expected of them and how they can achieve success. Teachers should provide clear criteria for assessment to help students understand the standards they are working toward. Use a variety of formative assessment techniques to monitor progress and provide constructive feedback, ensuring that all students feel supported in their learning journey. Adapting Strategies to Individual Needs

While these strategies have been proven effective, it is important to recognize that each student is unique. What works for one pupil may not work for another, and teachers must be flexible and adaptable in their approach. Sometimes, the simplest techniques can be the most effective, provided they are thoughtfully implemented with the needs of individual students in mind.

Inclusion, Equal Opportunities, and Legislative Context

The importance of inclusion in education is firmly rooted in legislative frameworks. Key milestones, such as the Sex Discrimination Act (1975), the Race Relations Act (1976), and the Report of Special Educational Needs (1978), have shaped the educational landscape by emphasizing the right of all students to an equitable curriculum. As Mitchell (2003, p. 19) states, "All students have a right to an entitlement curriculum regardless of sex, race, ethnicity, class, age, ability, special education needs, sexuality, physical impairment, religion, cultural, linguistic background, or other background aspects in which forms of discrimination might occur."

These legal foundations underscore the importance of addressing systemic barriers and ensuring that all students have access to high-quality education. In the context of MFL, this means creating a learning environment where every pupil, regardless of their background or ability, feels valued and supported.

Inclusion in the MFL classroom is not just a matter of equity—it is a fundamental component of effective teaching and learning. By implementing strategies such as thoughtful lesson planning, fostering positive teacher-pupil relationships, and using AFL practices, MFL teachers can create an environment where all students have the opportunity to succeed. This chapter has highlighted the importance of adapting strategies to meet the diverse needs of students and has emphasized the role of inclusion in promoting both academic achievement and personal growth. Through these efforts, MFL teachers can ensure that their classrooms are not only inclusive but also transformative spaces for learning and development.

Linguistic competence is just one part of MFL practice's impact. A child who feels like they belong in the classroom, a learner who gets a specialized path carved to achieve their excellence exudes confidence; not only in the classroom, but also on a global scale. This confidence translates into a powerful perception shift, making the playing field equal for those who may think that they are not capable. This shift helps them create better goals - aiding them in improving in all facets of life.

What educators also need to keep in their minds is that there are no fixed output from inclusion practice. MFL inclusion needs constant revision, input, adjustments, and improvements. As previously stated, inclusion practice requires planning and mapping according to the dynamic needs of the students in the classroom. What worked before may not work for another. It is keyto learn how to read a room, and MFL-skilled teachers become an expert in this realm. Inclusion not just includes linguistics. It accounts for social cues, needs of different children and understanding the intricacies of cultural sensitivities. This response is a goalpost for professional growth and successful inclusion.

Inclusion is deeply intertwined with the emotional climate of the classroom. An MFL classroom is a place where a student should feel most secure. They should be given the space to make mistakes, learn to take more risks, and have a close relationship with their peers and their teacher. These emotions are key in an MFL classroom that puts a spotlight on pronunciation, public speaking, and creative expression. This builds an excellent groundwork for the students to get comfortable with failing, and trying again.

Inclusive MFL education comes with various dimensions to it. Words carry emotion, not just in context, but also in their history, cultural significance, and emotional attachment. If a classroom that follows social norms, many marginalized students get left behind, fuelling the inequality and harbouring resentment in the classroom. Students who are a part of an inclusive classroom feel liberated and connect better with their peers and teachers. They not only feel welcomed, they feel celebrated.

Cognitive differences and Neurodivergence is currently on the top of development in teaching techniques in this generation. Historically, students with ADHD, Dyslexia, or Autism have been neglected and underserved in terms of linguistics learning. Research shows that when given resources to help them adapt (such as visual and auditory aids, dividing curriculum into digestible chunks, or creating personalized plans) can help these children thrive; bringing them up with all of the others. These teaching tools can also exhibit various unique perspectives, highlights strength, and makes students feel more confident in their classroom.

A critical part of inclusion is recognizing that a framework cannot exceed a **teacher's intentionality** with inclusion. Any checklist will only prove to be effective when it gets translated into the classroom every day. Inclusion is not just what gets taught, it also represents how it gets taught and what emotions felt during the process. A teacher needs to be vigilant in terms of adding inclusion in their classroom. They need to make sure that their inclusion reflects their intention – making everyone feel at home. The practices they need to adopt needs to make sure it includes diverse cultures, eliminates any microaggression, assumptions, or alienation.

Improvements can be made to the MFL inclusion classroom by gathering feedback from the students in your classroom. Students can often help a teacher to improve their teaching approach by pointing out what works and what doesn't. Students can better dictate what they feel in the classroom – where they are passing and where they are falling behind. They can give better feedback about their progress. Teachers can do learn from their students' voices via different mediums, such as self-reflection worksheets. Reflective journals, exit slips, and quick check ins by their teacher. This approach makes the students a co-creator of their own linguists' experience, where as teachers learn insightful feedback from their students in the process.

Integrating cultural conversations in the classroom is equally essential. With being a MFL teacher comes a unique opportunity to build intercultural understanding, while validating every student's culture. This inclusion makes them feel welcomed in the classroom while at the same time, they are questioning stereotypes, breaking down barriers of oppression, understanding history, and highlighting different legacies and cultures. Teachers can integrate cultures through various mediums including role play, idioms, phrases, and group assignments, where the students understand other cultures while comparing and reflecting on their own.

Working closely with parents and carers can really strengthen inclusion efforts in the MFL classroom. Families, especially in multilingual and multicultural settings, are often a powerful but underused resource in the learning process. For students, this bridge makes a big difference. It shows them that their identity and background are valued. When schools actively try to involve parents—by sending home translated newsletters, hosting multilingual support sessions, or celebrating different cultures through school events—it helps build a meaningful connection between home and school. In the context of learning a foreign language, this link is even more impactful, as it reinforces the idea that language isn't just something to study—it's something to live and experience.

Inclusion is best done when the teachers also feel supported. Collaboration is the backbone of professional development. Help and support from peers and leadership is crucial in this context. A teacher cannot build inclusion on their own, the entire organization needs to back them up as inclusion is a shared responsibility. As this chapter illuminated on the importance of collaboration from every aspect, inclusion is not just a criterion to be fulfilled, it is a moral imperative, a collective strength of students, teachers, peers, parents and leadership to build a hub for inclusion and growth to help the students flourish.

Chapter 2: Mentoring and Coaching in Education

Mentoring has long been recognized as a valuable strategy in the development of individuals across various fields, including education. While the role of mentoring in educational programs has recently been under increased scrutiny, the concept itself is far from new (Wallace & Gravells, 2007b; Megginson, Clutterbuck, Garvey, Stores, & Garret-Harris, 2006). The potential benefits of mentoring within educational contexts are well-documented, with research consistently associating the presence of a mentor with a range of positive career outcomes. For instance, protégés often achieve more promotions (Dreher & Ash, 1990; Scandura, 1992), earn higher incomes (Chao, Walz, & Gardner, 1992; Dreher & Ash, 1990; Whitley, Dougherty, & Dreher, 1991), report greater career mobility (Scandura, 1992), and express higher levels of career satisfaction (Fagenson, 1989) compared to those without mentors.

At its heart, mentoring is more than a professional arrangement—it is a human connection built on trust, empathy, and shared growth. The most impactful mentoring relationships often leave a lasting imprint not because of formal outcomes but because someone took the time to truly listen, guide, and believe in another's potential. In schools, where the demands of teaching can be relentless, a mentor who offers reassurance during moments of doubt or direction during times of uncertainty can make the difference between a teacher thriving or burning out.

As Clutterbuck (2004, p. 6) notes, "Employers' organizations have found that having a well-run mentoring scheme has a significant, positive impact upon both recruitment and retention." Thus, mentoring is not only an asset for individual development but also a significant tool for organizational success. This chapter aims to explore the positive effects and outcomes of mentoring while investigating how these outcomes may vary depending on the mentoring style and the nature of the relationship. The analysis draws on the work of key scholars, including Clutterbuck (1995, 2004, 2005, 2008), Wallace and Gravells (2005, 2007), and Megginson (2006).

In educational institutions, the ripple effects of mentoring extend beyond the mentor-mentee pair and contribute to the overall **school culture and climate**. When mentoring is embedded in the fabric of a school, it signals a commitment to professional learning, staff well-being, and continuous improvement. New teachers are more likely to feel welcomed, understood, and encouraged to grow, while experienced educators are given the opportunity to reflect on their own practice through guiding others. This exchange of experience and perspective fosters a collaborative ethos, reducing professional isolation and promoting interdependence among staff.

Furthermore, effective mentoring can be a powerful **vehicle for promoting equity and diversity in education**. By intentionally matching mentors and mentees across different backgrounds—whether by gender, race, age, or teaching subject—schools can challenge unconscious biases, widen professional networks, and create safe spaces for honest dialogue about identity and inclusion. For example, a mentee from an underrepresented group may find validation and motivation when working with a mentor who recognises and actively supports their unique challenges. Similarly, mentors benefit from exposure to different lived experiences, which can broaden their understanding and strengthen their own inclusive practices.

The emotional impact of mentoring should also not be underestimated. A strong mentoring relationship provides not just professional guidance but also **emotional anchoring**. For early-career teachers especially, the pressures of behaviour management, curriculum demands, and imposter syndrome can be overwhelming. A mentor who listens without judgment, offers reassurance, and helps reframe setbacks can become a vital source of resilience. Over time, this emotional support translates into greater confidence, reduced burnout, and a stronger sense of belonging within the school.

Research highlights several tangible outcomes that stem from successful mentoring schemes. These benefits apply to individual teachers, mentors, and the institution as a whole. Among the most commonly reported positive impacts are:

1. **Improved staff retention**, particularly among early-career teachers who feel supported in their transition.
2. **Greater job satisfaction** as teachers feel recognised, guided, and professionally developed.

3. **Enhanced teaching quality**, driven by reflective dialogue, feedback, and shared expertise.
4. **Increased collaboration and trust** across departments and year groups.
5. **Stronger leadership pipelines**, such as mentoring, often inspire future leaders to emerge and develop.
6. **Cultural inclusivity**, such as mentoring relationships, creates opportunities to challenge bias and promote diverse voices.

These outcomes reinforce the idea that mentoring is not a luxury or optional extra but a strategic investment in people and progress. When done well, mentoring becomes a cornerstone of educational excellence, bridging the gap between potential and performance.

Formal vs. Informal Mentoring

A fundamental distinction in mentoring lies between formal and informal relationships. Informal mentoring develops organically, often based on mutual interests or admiration, whereas formal mentoring is typically established through organizational intervention, such as pairing mentors and protégés through structured programs (Douglas, 1997). Another significant difference is the duration of the relationship; informal mentoring relationships often last longer, while formal arrangements are usually time-bound.

One of the challenges in studying informal mentoring is the difficulty in capturing "mentoring moments" that occur spontaneously and are, therefore, harder to document. These unplanned interactions often go unnoticed but can have profound impacts on the mentee. Formal mentoring, on the other hand, tends to be more structured, measurable, and aligned with specific organizational or educational goals. This chapter aims to clarify why formal mentoring may be more advantageous for mentees, mentors, and organizations alike.

While the focus of this chapter is on mentoring within educational frameworks, the insights presented here are broadly applicable across various sectors and disciplines. By exploring different mentoring styles and their effects, it is hoped that both researchers and readers will gain a deeper understanding of mentoring and how to leverage it effectively.

Choosing the Right Model for Schools

In an educational setting, choosing between formal and informal mentoring models should be informed by **context, purpose, and available resources**. Formal mentoring is often more practical for large institutions where structure, fairness, and accountability are critical—particularly when supporting new teachers or implementing whole-school improvement strategies. However, informal mentoring can flourish in schools with a strong culture of collaboration, where relationships evolve naturally and organically across departments.

Rather than viewing these models as mutually exclusive, many schools are now adopting **hybrid approaches** that blend structure with flexibility. For example, a formal induction program might assign new teachers a mentor while also encouraging wider networking and informal peer connections through coaching sessions or professional learning communities.

Key Features of a Hybrid Mentoring Approach

A blended mentoring model draws from the strengths of both formal and informal structures. The most effective hybrid systems often include:

1. **Clear roles and expectations** through formal agreements, training, and time allocation.
2. **Autonomy in relationship-building** allows mentees to seek support from others beyond their assigned mentor.
3. **Regular check-ins and feedback mechanisms** to track progress and adapt goals.
4. **Opportunities for reflection and dialogue** are often facilitated through informal conversations, joint planning, or shared CPD.

This flexible format ensures that while mentoring is supported institutionally, it also respects the personal nature of mentor-mentee dynamics.

Informal Mentoring: The Power of Authenticity

Informal mentoring is often where the deepest, most enduring professional relationships are formed. These mentorships grow out of **mutual respect, shared values, or even personal chemistry**. Teachers often remember these relationships not because they were assigned but because they were chosen—or emerged naturally out of collaboration, conversation, or a moment of vulnerability.

In this type of mentoring, there is often less pressure to "perform" and more space for authentic connection. Mentees may feel more comfortable asking questions, admitting doubts, or exploring unconventional teaching approaches. The learning is fluid, driven by curiosity rather than obligation. Though harder to measure, the **impact of informal mentoring is often more transformative**—fuelled by trust, empathy, and a sense of shared journey.

Formal Mentoring: The Value of Structure

Despite its more rigid format, formal mentoring offers **a level of consistency and equity** that is particularly valuable in diverse school settings. New teachers, especially those from underrepresented backgrounds or different educational systems, benefit from the clear scaffolding formal mentoring provides. Scheduled sessions, goal-setting, and documentation, can help ensure that critical support is not left to chance or reliant on informal social dynamics.

Formal mentoring also strengthens accountability and creates **a professional feedback loop**, allowing mentors to guide, evaluate, and model best practices within the school's framework. When supported by leadership, formal programs can improve teaching standards, support whole-school initiatives, and foster a culture of shared responsibility for professional growth.

Reimagining Mentoring for Modern Education

As schools continue to evolve, mentoring must also adapt to reflect new priorities: **inclusivity, staff well-being, digital fluency, and resilience** in the face of constant change. Effective mentoring today is less about hierarchy and more about partnership. Whether formal or informal, modern mentoring should be reciprocal, inclusive, and grounded in real-world challenges teachers face.

Mentoring in the 21st century might involve co-teaching, digital collaboration, mental health check-ins, or coaching around work-life balance. It might mean facilitating connections across roles—such as a senior leader mentoring a teaching assistant aiming to train as a teacher or an experienced classroom practitioner mentoring a middle leader on pedagogy. What remains constant is the need for **genuine human connection and a shared belief in each other's growth**.

Advantages and Disadvantages of Mentoring

The benefits of mentoring have been widely acknowledged for decades. As early as 1995, Hay highlighted the foundational concept of mentoring as one person passing their knowledge and wisdom to another. Wallace and Gravells (2007, p. 9) observed that "most of us, at one time or another, will have experienced the benefits of mentoring."

Clutterbuck (2004) identified several organizational benefits of well-structured mentoring programs, including improved recruitment and retention, more effective succession planning, support for employees during periods of major change, and increased productivity. More recently, Hobson, Ashby, Malderez, and Tomlinson (2009) added that mentoring positively affects organizations by fostering better relationships among staff, encouraging collaboration, and promoting professional development.

However, mentoring is not without its challenges. Several authors (Eby et al., 2004; Feldman, 1999; Hobson, 2008; Long, 1997; Scandura, 1998) have highlighted potential negative consequences, such as:

1. **For Mentees**: A mentoring relationship can sometimes undermine self-confidence, increase pressure and anxiety, or lead to dependency on the mentor.
2. **For Mentors**: Mentors may experience a sense of isolation, frustration, or a lack of reciprocal benefits from the relationship.

3. **For Organizations**: Ineffective mentoring programs may fail to challenge the status quo, becoming stagnant and unproductive.

Acknowledging these potential drawbacks is essential to ensuring that mentoring programs are designed and implemented in ways that maximize benefits while minimizing risks.

In the school environment, mentoring is often where personal and professional worlds intersect. It is not uncommon for mentors to become sounding boards for mentees navigating both classroom practice and wider life pressures. This dual role means mentoring has the potential to nurture not only better teaching but also greater well-being and resilience. Schools that encourage this culture of support often find it enhances staff morale and creates a more cohesive and motivated team.

Maximising Mentoring Impact Through Clear Structures

To ensure mentoring programs deliver their full potential, clear structures must be in place from the outset. A successful mentoring framework includes defined roles, expectations, timelines, and regular check-ins. Ambiguity in the mentoring process can lead to frustration or confusion, especially for new teachers who are still navigating the complexities of school culture and practice. When both mentor and mentee understand their objectives and boundaries, the mentoring relationship becomes more focused and productive.

Key elements of a well-structured mentoring program include:

1. A formalised induction and orientation process for mentees.
2. Training for mentors on active listening, feedback, and goal-setting.
3. Scheduled meeting times with clearly set agendas.

Monitoring mechanisms to assess progress and address emerging issues.

Emotional Intelligence in Mentoring Relationships

One of the most undervalued yet critical elements of successful mentoring is **emotional intelligence (EI)**. Mentors with high EI are better equipped to recognise when a mentee is struggling—academically or emotionally—and can respond with empathy, patience, and perspective. This emotional attunement helps to establish psychological safety, allowing mentees to be more open about their concerns and more receptive to feedback. In contrast, mentoring relationships that lack emotional intelligence can quickly become transactional, hierarchical, or strained.

Mentors with strong emotional intelligence demonstrate the following:

1. Empathy and active listening.
2. The ability to give constructive feedback without discouraging.
3. Sensitivity to the personal and professional pressures their mentees face.
4. A non-judgmental attitude that encourages growth and reflection.

The Risk of Mismatched Pairings

Despite the best intentions, not all mentoring pairings result in successful outcomes. Mismatched mentor-mentee pairs—whether due to personality clashes, differences in communication styles, or conflicting pedagogical philosophies—can hinder development rather than promote it. Poor alignment can lead to disengagement or even resentment, undermining the potential benefits of the program. To mitigate this risk, schools should allow opportunities for feedback and re-matching when necessary while also offering multiple avenues of informal support.

Indicators of an ineffective mentoring match may include:

1. Lack of communication or irregular meetings.
2. Persistent misunderstandings or misaligned expectations.
3. A noticeable absence of trust or rapport.
4. The mentee expressing reluctance to seek support or raise concerns

Sustaining Mentoring Over Time

While many mentoring programs focus on the induction year, there is growing recognition that **mentoring should be sustained beyond the early stages** of a teacher's career. Ongoing mentoring supports teachers as they face new responsibilities, transitions into leadership, or challenges related to curriculum changes and educational reforms. By expanding mentoring opportunities throughout a teacher's career lifecycle, schools can promote retention, reinvigorate professional learning, and build leadership capacity from within.

Long-term mentoring benefits include:

1. Support for career progression and leadership development.
2. Space for continued reflection and innovation in teaching practice.
3. Greater job satisfaction and professional resilience.
4. Stronger intergenerational collaboration within staff teams.

Embedding a Mentoring Culture in Schools

For mentoring to be fully effective, it must evolve from a stand-alone initiative into **a whole-school culture**. This means promoting mentoring not just as a support mechanism for new teachers but as a core strategy for professional development and staff well-being. When mentoring is embedded in school ethos—supported by leadership, prioritised in timetables, and aligned with school improvement goals—it can become a driver of sustainable change and collective efficacy.

Steps to embed a mentoring culture include:

1. Recognising and rewarding the role of mentors in staff appraisal systems.
2. Encouraging cross-departmental mentoring to build interdisciplinary links.
3. Aligning mentoring goals with whole-school development plans.
4. Creating time and space for reflective practice across all career stages.

Mentoring Styles and Functions

Kram's mentor role theory (1985) identifies four key functions of mentoring, all of which contribute to the mentee's development:

1. Acceptance and Confirmation: Helping the mentee develop a sense of professional identity and self-worth.
2. Counselling: Providing problem-solving support and guidance.
3. Friendship: Offering respect, empathy, and emotional support.
4. Role Modelling: Serving as an example for the mentee to emulate.

Clutterbuck, as cited by Wallace and Gravells (2007), categorizes mentoring styles along a continuum from directive to non-directive. These styles include:

Directive styles: Such as the roles of coach or caretaker, where the mentor takes a hands-on approach.

Non-directive styles: Such are the roles of facilitator or counsellor, where the mentor encourages the mentee to take the lead in their own development.

The effectiveness of each style depends on the context and the individual needs of the mentee.

Formal vs. Informal Mentoring: Advantages and Disadvantages

Formal and informal mentoring each has unique benefits and challenges. Informal mentoring, for example, often develops based on mutual identification, shared interests, or perceived competencies (Erikson, 1963; Kram, 1985a). Protégés tend to select mentors they admire, while mentors often choose high-performing protégés who show promise. These relationships are typically characterized by a strong interpersonal connection, which fosters trust and a deeper commitment to the mentoring process.

In contrast, formal mentoring programs are designed to ensure that all individuals have access to mentoring, regardless of their ability to form informal relationships. Formal programs provide structure, clear objectives, and measurable outcomes, making them particularly beneficial in organizational settings. However, formal mentoring relationships may lack the natural rapport and longevity of informal ones.

As Wallace and Gravells (2006) observe, "We instinctively tolerate a greater degree of challenge from someone who we feel is supportive, wants us to succeed, and has our interests at heart." Regardless of the format, the success of a mentoring relationship ultimately depends on the quality of the connection between mentor and mentee.

Mentoring is a powerful tool for fostering personal and professional growth, both within education and beyond. While formal and informal mentoring each has its advantages and disadvantages, both play a crucial role in supporting mentees, mentors, and organizations. By understanding the various mentoring styles and their impacts, educators and organizations can design mentoring programs that maximize benefits and minimize challenges. As this chapter has demonstrated, mentoring is not a one-size-fits-all process; it is a dynamic relationship that must be tailored to the needs of the individuals and the context in which it occurs.

As educational environments continue to diversify, the need for **adaptive and responsive mentoring practices** becomes even more critical. Today's mentors must be equipped to support colleagues from a range of backgrounds, experiences, and identities. This includes understanding how cultural norms, communication preferences, and socio-political contexts may influence how mentoring is perceived and received. Mentoring programs that acknowledge and embrace this diversity are more likely to foster inclusive professional communities where everyone feels a sense of belonging and possibility.

In many ways, the most effective mentoring relationships—whether formal or informal—are those grounded in **shared purpose and reciprocal growth**. While the mentee may gain knowledge, skills, and confidence, the mentor too often reports increased reflection, renewed passion, and deeper insight into their own practice. This mutual benefit transforms mentoring from a top-down model into a two-way exchange that builds professional capital across the organisation. Schools that recognise mentoring as a collaborative endeavour are more likely to see lasting cultural and instructional improvement.

Ultimately, the goal of any mentoring initiative should be to build capacity—not dependency. A well-mentored teacher should leave the experience with not only improved skills but also the tools and confidence to mentor others. This cascading effect strengthens the entire educational ecosystem, creating a sustainable cycle of professional learning and support. Whether through structured programs or organic relationships, mentoring remains one of the most human and impactful forms of development available in education—an investment not only in practice but in people.

Chapter 3: Management in Teaching and Learning

The role of teacher assistants (TAs) in education has evolved significantly over time, with both positive and critical perspectives emerging about their impact on teaching and learning. Under the previous UK government, the value of teacher assistants was widely acknowledged, with research highlighting their contribution to raising student achievement (Balshaw & Farrell, 2002; HMI, 2002). However, more recent reports under the coalition government have raised concerns about the potential for support staff to have a negative impact in certain contexts (Blatchford et al., 2010; Emira, 2011).

Teacher assistants, often referred to by different designations depending on their roles and qualifications, contribute in varying ways to the learning environment. For instance, TAs are primarily tasked with providing substantial support within classrooms, while High-Level Teaching Assistants (HLTAs) may take on additional responsibilities, including duties outside the classroom (Drake et al., 2004; Townsend & Parker, 2009). These distinctions highlight the need for clarity and effective management to maximize their contributions to teaching and learning.

This diversity in roles among teaching assistants underscores both the complexity and the potential of their contribution to education. Teacher assistants are no longer simply helpers performing routine tasks; they are pivotal players in the educational ecosystem. Their presence can transform the classroom dynamic, offering personalized attention that teachers—often managing large classes—may struggle to provide consistently. From supporting individual students who face learning challenges to facilitating group activities, TAs serve as vital bridges between the teacher's objectives and the varied needs of pupils.

The role of High-Level Teaching Assistants (HLTAs), in particular, demonstrates the evolving nature of support staff in schools. HLTAs often act with a degree of autonomy, delivering lessons, managing small groups, or even leading entire classes when necessary. Their advanced training and broader responsibilities mean that they frequently engage in tasks that overlap with those traditionally reserved for qualified teachers. This development reflects a growing recognition that effective education demands a team approach—one where each member's skills are leveraged to foster a rich, inclusive learning environment.

However, this expanding scope of duties also raises important questions about professional identity and boundaries. Without clear role definitions and effective management, there is a risk of overlap or confusion, which can diminish both efficiency and morale. Teachers might feel their professional space is encroached upon, while TAs might be uncertain about their limits or undervalued for their contributions. This makes it essential for school leadership to establish transparent structures that define responsibilities, encourage collaboration, and promote mutual respect between all educational staff.

Moreover, the impact of teacher assistants extends beyond the classroom walls. Their involvement in extracurricular activities, administrative duties, and pastoral care highlights their integral role within the broader school community. By supporting students' social and emotional development alongside academic progress, TAs help build a nurturing environment where pupils feel safe, supported, and motivated. This holistic approach aligns with contemporary educational philosophies that value the development of the whole child, recognizing that academic success is closely linked to emotional well-being and a sense of belonging.

Investment in the professional development of teaching assistants is therefore not just beneficial—it is imperative. High-quality training equips TAs with the knowledge and confidence to handle complex educational needs, including supporting students with special educational needs and disabilities (SEND), English as an additional language (EAL), or behavioural challenges. Ongoing development opportunities also foster a culture of continuous learning among TAs, empowering them to stay current with best practices and educational innovations. In turn, this positively influences their effectiveness and satisfaction in the role.

Effective management of TAs also involves fostering a collaborative culture. When teachers and teaching assistants work closely as partners, sharing insights and strategies, the overall quality of teaching improves. Regular communication ensures that support is aligned with lesson objectives, providing students with consistent and coherent learning experiences. Collaborative planning sessions, joint professional development, and informal exchanges all contribute to building trust and respect, which are fundamental to a successful working relationship.

In conclusion, teaching assistants and HLTAs are indispensable members of the educational team. Their evolving roles offer exciting possibilities for enriching the learning environment, provided they are managed with clarity, respect, and strategic foresight. As education continues to adapt to diverse student needs and increasing demands on teachers, the role of teaching assistants will only grow in importance. By investing in their development and integrating them effectively into school leadership and teaching structures, schools can harness their full potential—ultimately enhancing outcomes for all learners.

Kramen (2008) outlined the responsibilities of teacher assistants across four key levels:

At the pupil level: Understanding and responding to pupils' learning and physical needs, encouraging independence, and providing rewards and praise.

At the teacher level: Supporting the preparation and maintenance of the learning environment, monitoring and evaluating pupil progress, and offering feedback on learning and behaviour.

At the school level: Functioning as team members and contributing to the broader school community.

At the curriculum level: Understanding learning theories, the National Curriculum, and national literacy and numeracy strategies.

The primary purpose of this chapter is to evaluate the positive effects and outcomes of having teacher assistants in educational settings and to explore whether they can be managed more effectively to enhance teaching and learning. This analysis draws on insights from Law and Glover's work, where they argue that "leaders and managers accomplish little on their own without the role and contributions of followers" (Law & Glover, 2000).

Understanding the positive impact of teacher assistants (TAs) requires a closer look at the dynamics of teamwork and leadership within educational settings. Law and Glover's insight reminds us that successful leadership is not about top-down commands but about harnessing the collective strengths of every individual involved. In this context, TAs are far more than passive supporters; they are active contributors whose engagement and expertise can significantly shape the learning experience.

Effective management of TAs begins with recognizing their unique position within the classroom. Unlike teachers, who carry the ultimate responsibility for curriculum delivery and assessment, TAs often have the advantage of working closely with individual students or small groups. This proximity allows them to identify subtle learning barriers, adapt support strategies in real-time, and build trusting relationships with pupils who may otherwise feel overlooked. When managed well, this can lead to measurable improvements in student confidence, engagement, and achievement.

Moreover, the value of TAs extends to supporting inclusive education. With increasing awareness and legal requirements surrounding special educational needs and disabilities (SEND), TAs play a crucial role in ensuring that all students have equitable access to learning opportunities. Their specialized knowledge and patient, personalized support help bridge gaps between diverse learners and the curriculum. As such, TAs are key players in schools' efforts to meet statutory inclusion mandates and promote diversity.

However, the full potential of teacher assistants can only be realized through strategic leadership and management. This requires school leaders to move beyond seeing TAs as auxiliary staff and instead view them as integral members of the educational team. Such a perspective demands investment in their professional development, clear communication channels, and inclusive decision-making processes. When TAs are involved in planning and reflective practice alongside teachers, their insights enrich instructional design and classroom management.

Research indicates that schools with well-integrated TAs report higher overall staff morale and a more cohesive teaching culture. This is no coincidence. When teachers and TAs respect each other's expertise and collaborate effectively, they create a positive work environment that benefits everyone. This atmosphere fosters creativity, problem-solving, and shared responsibility—qualities that are essential in today's complex educational landscape.

Conversely, neglecting to properly manage TAs can have detrimental effects. Poor role definition, lack of training, or exclusion from school activities can leave TAs feeling undervalued and disconnected. This not only impacts their motivation but can also hinder the learning support provided to students. Furthermore, an over-reliance on TAs without adequate teacher involvement risks creating dependency rather than promoting student independence. Therefore, balance is critical.

Another important consideration is the evolving role of TAs amid educational reforms and increasing accountability measures. As schools face mounting pressures to raise standards and meet diverse learners' needs, TAs are often called upon to take on more complex duties. This trend underscores the necessity for leadership to ensure that TAs are not only equipped with the right skills but also supported emotionally and professionally. Regular supervision, feedback, and recognition contribute to their confidence and effectiveness.

In summary, the benefits of teacher assistants in educational settings are clear: they enhance individualised support, promote inclusion, and strengthen the teaching team. However, unlocking these benefits hinges on effective leadership that values their role, invests in their growth, and fosters collaborative working cultures. As Law and Glover emphasize, no leader can succeed without the commitment and contribution of followers. In schools, TAs represent a vital part of this collective effort, and when managed thoughtfully, their impact on teaching and learning is profound and lasting.

Leadership and Management of Teacher Assistants

Leadership plays a vital role in shaping the effectiveness of teacher assistants. Effective leadership in managing teacher assistants requires a shift from traditional hierarchical models to more inclusive and participative approaches. Leaders who adopt transformational or distributed leadership styles create environments where TAs feel empowered and valued. These leadership styles encourage collaboration, open communication, and shared decision-making, enabling TAs to contribute their unique insights and skills. By fostering a culture of trust and respect, leaders can enhance TAs' motivation and commitment, which directly impacts classroom dynamics and student outcomes.

Leadership styles that are overly autocratic or top-down, fail to engage individuals in decision-making, and risk undermining group effectiveness and collaboration (Van Vugt et al., 2008). As Mastrangelo et al. (2004) emphasize, failing to share authority, even to a limited degree, can be highly detrimental to morale.

Teacher assistants, by virtue of their role in supporting classroom teachers, inevitably contribute to classroom management. Whether or not they actively exercise leadership, TAs and HLTAs must understand leadership styles and skills to participate effectively in educational settings (Kramen, 2008). Leadership, as Muijs and Harris (2003) and Watkinson (2003, p. 22) assert, does not solely reside with headteachers or senior leaders—it is distributed among all individuals with responsibilities.

Moreover, professional development tailored to leadership and management skills is essential for teacher assistants themselves. Training that includes conflict resolution, communication, and decision-making not only strengthens TAs' confidence but also equips them to take on leadership roles within the classroom and school community. When TAs are prepared to lead activities or support peer collaboration effectively, they transition from being mere assistants to influential facilitators of learning. This professional growth contributes to a more dynamic, responsive educational environment.

When teacher assistants are undervalued or overlooked, the quality of teaching, learning, and pupil achievement can suffer. Conversely, when TAs feel respected and are allowed to express their views, lead activities, and apply management skills, both practice and achievement improve. This chapter argues that engaging TAs in meaningful ways can unlock their potential and contribute significantly to the overall success of the school.

Importantly, school leaders must actively involve TAs in strategic conversations and school-wide initiatives to harness their full potential. Including TAs in staff meetings, curriculum planning, and feedback sessions demonstrates respect and acknowledges their critical role beyond routine classroom support. This inclusive approach not only improves morale but also leads to innovative practices and solutions born from diverse perspectives. By valuing TAs as partners rather than subordinates, schools create a unified team dedicated to enhancing educational quality and student success.

The Role of School Leaders

The attitude of school leaders toward teacher assistants is a critical factor in their effective management and deployment. Leaders who recognize the skills and potential of their support staff and trust their abilities are more likely to deploy them creatively and effectively (Law & Glover, 2000). This involves not only assigning tasks appropriately but also providing guidance, training, and opportunities for professional development (Watkinson, 2003).

School leaders and classroom teachers who actively engage TAs in the professional environment often find that their own management skills improve as a result (Law & Glover, 2000). This highlights the reciprocal nature of effective management: when leaders invest in their support staff, the entire teaching and learning environment benefits.

School leaders hold a pivotal role not only in setting the vision for their institutions but also in shaping the day-to-day experiences of teacher assistants (TAs) and the wider school community. Their attitudes and actions toward TAs can significantly influence the assistants' job satisfaction, professional growth, and ultimately, their effectiveness in supporting student learning. Leaders who view TAs as valuable colleagues and integral members of the educational team create a culture of respect and collaboration that permeates the entire school. This culture fosters greater cohesion, encourages open communication, and drives collective responsibility for student outcomes.

Effective school leaders understand that empowering TAs requires more than just assigning tasks; it involves cultivating an environment where support staff feel confident to contribute ideas, take initiative, and develop professionally. By actively involving TAs in decision-making processes—whether related to classroom strategies, behaviour management, or inclusive practices—leaders tap into a wealth of practical experience and diverse perspectives. This inclusion not only enhances the quality of educational provision but also strengthens TAs' sense of belonging and ownership within the school. Consequently, empowered TAs are more motivated and better equipped to adapt to the varying and complex needs of learners.

Professional development is a cornerstone of this empowerment. School leaders who prioritize ongoing training and learning opportunities for TAs demonstrate a commitment to their growth and the broader mission of the school. High-quality professional development programs tailored specifically to the diverse roles of TAs enable them to expand their skills in areas such as differentiated instruction, communication with students, behaviour support, and use of educational technology. Furthermore, leadership training for TAs who aspire to take on higher-level responsibilities can nurture future leaders within the school community, creating sustainable pathways for career progression and staff retention.

In addition to formal training, mentorship and coaching provided by school leaders and experienced teachers play a crucial role in developing TAs' competencies. Regular feedback sessions, reflective practice, and collaborative planning allow TAs to refine their skills and align their efforts closely with teaching goals. This ongoing dialogue builds trust and mutual respect, transforming the working relationship from one of supervision to partnership. When TAs feel heard and supported, they are more likely to contribute creatively to lesson delivery and pupil support, enhancing overall classroom effectiveness.

Another vital aspect of effective leadership is ensuring that the workload and deployment of TAs are balanced and strategic. Leaders must be mindful not to overburden TAs with administrative tasks or responsibilities outside their remit, which can detract from their core function of supporting teaching and learning. Instead, TAs should be deployed thoughtfully to maximize their impact—whether that means working with individuals who need targeted support, facilitating group work, or assisting with curriculum adaptation. Clear role definitions, combined with flexibility to meet emerging needs, help optimize the contributions of TAs without leading to burnout or role confusion.

The reciprocal benefits of investing in TAs extend beyond the assistants themselves. School leaders often find that when TAs are well-supported and integrated into the professional environment, the entire teaching team benefits from increased collaboration, reduced teacher workload, and enhanced classroom management. This positive synergy contributes to a more inclusive and responsive educational setting, where all staff members work collectively to meet the diverse needs of students. Ultimately, by valuing and developing teacher assistants, school leaders foster a culture of excellence and continuous improvement that drives school success.

The role of school leaders in managing and deploying TAs effectively cannot be overstated. Leadership that recognizes the unique skills of TAs, invests in their professional development, and includes them as key contributors within the school community not only enhances the assistants' effectiveness but also elevates the quality of teaching and learning across the institution. Through visionary, compassionate, and inclusive leadership, schools can unlock the full potential of their support staff, creating vibrant, dynamic environments where every learner has the opportunity to thrive.

Advantages and Disadvantages of Teacher Assistants

The integration of teacher assistants into classrooms has grown significantly in recent years. Kedney (1999) noted that the number of TA posts increased dramatically between 1996 and 1999, reflecting their growing importance in educational delivery teams.

Advantages

1. **Flexibility**: TAs provide additional support that allows teachers to focus on core instructional responsibilities.
2. **Individualized Support**: TAs can work closely with pupils who require additional help, tailoring their support to individual needs.
3. **Team Collaboration**: TAs contribute to a collaborative teaching environment, supporting teachers and other staff in achieving shared goals.

Disadvantages

4. **Dependence on TAs**: Over-reliance on TAs may inadvertently diminish the role of the teacher in certain aspects of classroom management and instruction.
5. **Inconsistent Training**: Variability in TA training and qualifications can lead to inconsistencies in their effectiveness.
6. **Resource Allocation**: Employing TAs requires significant financial investment, which may raise questions about cost-effectiveness, particularly in budget-constrained educational settings.

Improving the Management of Teacher Assistants

To address these challenges, educational leaders must adopt a strategic approach to managing TAs. This includes:

1. **Providing Comprehensive Training**: Ensuring that TAs have access to high-quality training that equips them with the knowledge and skills needed to excel in their roles.
2. **Fostering Collaboration**: Encouraging regular communication and collaboration between teachers and TAs to align their efforts and maximize their impact.
3. **Recognizing Contributions**: Valuing the contributions of TAs by including them in decision-making processes and acknowledging their achievements.

Leaders with successful deployment strategies often rely on high-quality guidance, targeted training, and ongoing professional development to optimise the role of Teaching Assistants (TAs) within the school community (Watkinson, 2003). Rather than viewing TAs as supplementary or peripheral staff, effective leaders see them as integral partners in the teaching and learning process. This involves not only clearly defining their responsibilities but also investing in their skills, confidence, and professional identity. When school leadership commits to training TAs in classroom management, subject-specific support, and inclusive education practices, TAs are better equipped to make meaningful contributions to pupil progress. Furthermore, by making strategic use of management skills both inside and outside the classroom—such as in planning sessions, behaviour interventions, and curriculum support—schools can foster a collaborative culture where all staff members, including TAs, feel empowered, respected, and motivated. This sense of professional value not only improves staff morale but also has a direct impact on student outcomes, as learners benefit from more cohesive, responsive, and supportive teaching teams.

The effective management of teacher assistants is essential to improving the quality of teaching and learning in schools. When TAs are well-managed, they can play a pivotal role in supporting pupils, teachers, and the broader school community. However, this requires school leaders to adopt inclusive and collaborative leadership styles, provide appropriate training and support, and recognize the value of TAs' contributions.

While the benefits of having teaching assistants in classrooms are undeniable, it is crucial to acknowledge and proactively address the challenges that accompany their deployment. One of the most significant challenges lies in the potential for role ambiguity and inconsistency in how TAs are utilized across different schools or even within the same institution. Without clear role definitions and boundaries, TAs may find themselves either underutilized or assigned tasks that do not fully leverage their skills and expertise. This can lead to frustration, diminished job satisfaction, and missed opportunities for meaningful student support. Additionally, inconsistencies in training and professional development can create wide variations in TA effectiveness, making it harder for schools to maintain a consistently high standard of support.

Another challenge is the risk of over-reliance on TAs to compensate for wider systemic issues, such as teacher workload or insufficient staffing. While TAs provide invaluable assistance, they should not be seen as a substitute for qualified teachers but as complementary professionals whose roles enhance, rather than replace, teacher-led instruction. Balancing this dynamic requires thoughtful leadership to ensure that TAs are deployed strategically, with clear goals and in ways that genuinely advance student learning. Furthermore, without proper support and inclusion in the school's pedagogical framework, TAs may struggle to feel fully integrated into the educational community, limiting their potential impact.

Fostering a culture of collaboration and shared leadership is essential to overcoming these challenges. When school leaders cultivate an environment where TAs are valued partners rather than peripheral helpers, the entire teaching team benefits. This culture encourages open communication, mutual respect, and shared responsibility for student outcomes. Collaborative planning, regular team meetings, and joint professional development opportunities can break down barriers between teachers and TAs, promoting alignment in instructional strategies and behaviour management approaches. Empowered TAs who feel trusted and included are more likely to take initiative, contribute innovative ideas, and respond flexibly to student needs.

Moreover, shared leadership models that distribute decision-making responsibilities help build collective ownership of the school's educational goals. By involving TAs in discussions around curriculum adaptations, inclusion strategies, and classroom management policies, leaders tap into the rich insights that TAs gain from their close work with pupils. This inclusive approach not only enhances the quality of support provided but also fosters a sense of professional identity and belonging among TAs. When TAs perceive their contributions as meaningful and valued, motivation and morale improve, which positively influences their effectiveness and retention.

Ultimately, addressing the challenges associated with TA deployment requires intentional leadership that views TAs as integral members of the educational team. Through clear role definition, targeted training, strategic deployment, and a collaborative culture grounded in shared leadership, schools can maximize the impact of TAs on pupil achievement. This holistic approach ensures that the potential of teaching assistants is fully realized, enriching teaching and learning experiences and contributing to improved outcomes for all students.

Chapter 4: Innovations in Teaching and Learning

The integration of innovative technologies, such as wikis, into educational programs, has become an increasingly significant area of focus within the field of teaching and learning. While the use of wikis in education is now under heightened scrutiny, the concept itself is not new (Vickery, 2007; Adie, 2006; Alexander, 2006). The potential benefits of wikis in the classroom are well-documented, with research highlighting their capacity to transform collaborative learning environments. According to Leuf and Cunningham (2001), a wiki is defined as a "...collection of interlinked web pages, a hypertext system for storing and modifying information, a database, where each page is easily edited by any user with a form-capable web browser client" (p. 14).

Wikis stand out among digital tools for their unique ability to democratize knowledge creation and foster a culture of collaboration among learners. Unlike traditional learning resources, which often position students as passive recipients of information, wikis invite active participation, making every user both a contributor and editor. This open, participatory approach aligns closely with contemporary educational theories that emphasize constructivism—where learners build understanding through interaction and shared experiences. In this way, wikis transform the classroom into a vibrant learning community, where knowledge is not fixed but continuously evolving.

The editable nature of wikis encourages students to engage critically with content rather than merely consuming it. Learners are challenged to assess, revise, and expand information collaboratively, which deepens their understanding and develops important skills such as critical thinking, digital literacy, and communication. This ongoing process of negotiation and consensus-building mirrors real-world knowledge production and helps prepare students for active citizenship in an increasingly interconnected and information-rich society.

Moreover, wikis facilitate peer learning by creating spaces where students can learn from one another's insights and feedback. This peer-to-peer interaction often leads to increased motivation and a greater sense of ownership over the learning process. For many students, the opportunity to contribute to a shared digital product can boost confidence and encourage risk-taking in language use or subject-specific discussions, particularly in environments where mistakes are viewed as part of learning. When learners see their edits and additions reflected in a collective work, they experience a tangible sense of contribution and accomplishment.

From the teacher's perspective, wikis offer a versatile tool to support diverse pedagogical goals. They can be used for collaborative writing projects, research assignments, revision activities, or as digital portfolios showcasing student progress. Wikis also provide transparency, allowing educators to monitor individual participation and identify both strengths and areas where students may need additional support. This real-time insight can inform timely intervention and personalized feedback, helping to bridge gaps in understanding and foster continuous improvement.

However, the implementation of wikis is not without its challenges. Teachers must carefully scaffold wiki activities to ensure that collaboration is structured and purposeful. Clear guidelines regarding editing rights, content expectations, and group roles are essential to prevent common pitfalls such as unequal participation or conflicts over content ownership. Additionally, some students may initially struggle with the technical aspects or the shift in responsibility that wikis demand, necessitating initial training and ongoing support.

Despite these hurdles, the adaptability of wikis allows them to complement traditional teaching methods rather than replace them. When integrated thoughtfully, wikis can enhance student engagement, deepen learning, and cultivate essential 21st-century skills. They also align with the increasing emphasis on learner autonomy and personalized learning paths, as students can contribute at their own pace and according to their interests.

As educational institutions continue to explore the potential of technology-enhanced learning, wikis represent a compelling example of how digital innovation can support more interactive, inclusive, and student-centred classrooms. Their capacity to transform static content into dynamic, collaboratively constructed knowledge makes them a powerful tool in the ongoing evolution of teaching and learning practices.

Wikis are also considered a fundamental component of Web 2.0, the emergent generation of web tools and applications that enhance collaboration and user engagement (Jonassen, Peck, & Wilson, 1999). A key feature of wikis is their capacity to actively involve users in the construction of their own knowledge (Boulos, Maramba, & Wheeler, 2006).

The purpose of this chapter is twofold: first, to explore the positive effects and outcomes of using wikis in the classroom, and second, to determine whether wikis can enhance student motivation in the context of Modern Foreign Languages (MFL) education. The chapter seeks to address the following questions: Can the principles of wikis be effectively applied in a typical secondary education setting? Will students find wikis valuable? Can wikis promote motivation in learning MFL?

This chapter draws on the foundational work of prominent scholars such as Leuf and Cunningham (2001), Adie (2006), and Alexander (2006) to thoroughly examine the transformative potential of wikis as innovative tools for teaching and learning. Leuf and Cunningham, who are credited with pioneering the original wiki concept, provide essential insights into the technical and philosophical underpinnings of wikis, highlighting their capacity to create collaborative, user-driven knowledge spaces. Their work illustrates how wikis break down traditional barriers in information sharing, enabling learners and educators to become active participants in the co-construction of knowledge rather than passive consumers.

Adie's research (2006) offers a practical exploration of how wikis function within educational settings, emphasizing their role in fostering student engagement and collaboration. Adie investigates how wikis encourage learner autonomy by providing a flexible platform where students can contribute, edit, and reflect on their learning in real time. This work highlights the pedagogical shifts that wikis introduce—moving away from teacher-centred instruction toward more learner-centred approaches, where students take greater ownership of their educational journeys.

Alexander (2006) extends this discussion by contextualizing wikis within broader educational technology trends, considering both the opportunities and challenges they present. Alexander's analysis draws attention to the social constructivist theories that underpin wiki use, positioning them as tools that support social interaction, dialogue, and critical thinking—core components of meaningful learning experiences. He also acknowledges the need for thoughtful implementation, cautioning that without appropriate guidance and support, the collaborative potential of wikis may not be fully realized.

Together, these scholars provide a comprehensive framework that informs the chapter's exploration of wikis in Modern Foreign Language (MFL) education. Their combined insights help to unravel the multifaceted benefits of wikis—including enhanced collaboration, increased motivation, and development of digital literacy skills—while also addressing the practical considerations necessary for effective integration into curricula. By building on this rich scholarly foundation, the chapter aims to offer educators a nuanced understanding of how wikis can be leveraged to enrich teaching and learning practices in today's increasingly digital and interconnected classrooms.

Origins and Development of Wikis

The concept of the wiki, though now widely familiar, was once a groundbreaking innovation in digital communication. Among the most prominent and influential examples is **Wikipedia**—a global online initiative launched in 2001 with the ambitious aim of creating a free, user-generated encyclopaedia accessible in multiple languages. Within just three years, it had already surpassed 1.5 million articles, outpacing all traditional encyclopaedias and establishing itself as the largest open-content project in the world (Vob, 2005). This remarkable growth was not driven by a single organisation or editorial team, but by a vast network of volunteers contributing, editing, and refining content in real time.

The success of Wikipedia underscores the revolutionary potential of wikis: their ability to harness collective knowledge, promote democratic participation, and break down traditional barriers to information sharing. Unlike static websites or top-down knowledge platforms, wikis invite collaboration, adaptability, and continuous improvement. In educational contexts, this model offers exciting possibilities—not only for accessing information but for **actively**

creating and shaping it, making learners participants in, rather than just consumers of, knowledge.

The term "wiki" originates from the Hawaiian word meaning "fast" (Bergin, 2002). The original software, "WikiWiki," was formally launched by Jimmy Wales and Larry Sanger in 2001, building on the pioneering work of Ward Cunningham. The goal was to create a simple, effective tool for knowledge management and online collaboration (Cunningham et al., 2001).

In the context of education, wikis offer a platform for learners to collaborate on projects, share ideas, and construct knowledge as a team. This chapter explores how wikis can be used to engage students in active, computer-supported collaborative work, aligning with the principles of A^3—anytime, anywhere, and anybody (Holzinger, 2002).

Advantages and Disadvantages of Wikis in MFL

One significant advantage of using wikis in the classroom is their popularity as a teaching and learning tool. Wikis provide a collaborative space where students can edit and build project pages together in real time, fostering a sense of ownership and teamwork (Jonassen et al., 2008).

However, integrating wikis into the curriculum presents several challenges, especially within the context of Modern Foreign Languages (MFL) education. Although wikis have been successfully implemented in disciplines such as history, science, and social studies—where collaborative research and content creation align naturally with subject goals—their application in language learning is still relatively underexplored. The limited research available, as noted by Castaneda (2007), points to a significant gap in understanding how wikis can be tailored to support the unique demands of MFL classrooms. These demands include fostering linguistic accuracy, encouraging oral and written communication skills, and addressing diverse learner proficiency levels.

One of the main challenges lies in designing wiki-based activities that effectively integrate language acquisition goals without overwhelming students with the technical or collaborative aspects of the platform. Language learners may require additional scaffolding to navigate wiki editing tools, especially when they are simultaneously grappling with new vocabulary, grammar, and cultural nuances. This dual cognitive load can make wiki tasks more demanding than traditional assignments, potentially discouraging participation if not carefully managed. Moreover, maintaining quality control and linguistic accuracy within a collaborative, open-editing environment can be difficult, necessitating active teacher involvement to monitor and guide contributions.

Another significant challenge is ensuring equitable participation among students. Wikis depend on collaborative input, but without clear roles or motivation, some students may contribute less, while others dominate the content creation process. This imbalance can undermine both the learning outcomes and the sense of shared ownership that wikis aim to foster. Furthermore, the asynchronous and often remote nature of wiki collaboration requires effective communication skills and self-regulation, which may vary widely among language learners.

The scarcity of focused studies on wiki use in MFL settings also means that educators often lack practical frameworks or evidence-based strategies to guide their implementation. Questions remain about how wikis can best support the development of key language skills, such as speaking and listening, which traditionally rely on real-time interaction. Additionally, considerations around assessment practices, feedback mechanisms, and integration with existing curriculum standards need further investigation to ensure that wiki activities are meaningful and measurable.

This gap in the literature underscores the importance of continued research into both the pedagogical affordances and the potential pitfalls of wikis in language education. By exploring student experiences, learning outcomes, and teacher perspectives, future studies can help identify best practices for incorporating wikis in MFL classrooms. Such research will contribute to the development of more effective, engaging, and inclusive digital learning environments that harness the collaborative power of wikis while addressing the specific challenges of language acquisition.

Addressing Key Issues in MFL Learning

Noam Chomsky (1986, 1998, 2006) identified two key challenges in language learning:

Vocabulary Learning Issues – The difficulty of acquiring and retaining new vocabulary.

Processing Vocabulary Limitations – The challenge learners face in processing and using new vocabulary effectively.

Chomsky further distinguished between two types of learning:

General Learning (Empiricism): Collecting linguistic data from the environment.

Specific Language Learning (Nativism): Developing competence in specific languages.

The use of wikis in the classroom has the potential to address these challenges by providing a collaborative platform for vocabulary acquisition and retention.

Catering to Different Learning Styles

Fleming's VARK learning style theory (1991) identifies four distinct learning preferences:

1. **Visual**: Learners who benefit from images and visual representations.
2. **Auditory**: Learners who prefer spoken explanations and discussions.
3. **Read/Write**: Learners who excel through reading and writing activities.
4. **Kinaesthetic**: Learners who learn best through hands-on activities and physical engagement.

According to Fleming (2011), effective teaching strategies should cater to all four learning styles. Wikis provide a versatile platform that can accommodate diverse preferences:

1. **Visual Learners**: Can design and interact with visually appealing wiki pages.

2. **Auditory Learners**: Can engage in discussions and audio-supported tasks embedded in the wiki.
3. **Read/Write Learners**: Can contribute written content and review others' work.
4. **Kinaesthetic Learners**: Can actively participate in the creation and editing of wiki content.

By addressing these varied learning styles, wikis have the potential to make language learning more inclusive and effective.

In conclusion, wikis present a unique and powerful platform that fosters collaboration, interactivity, and active participation, making them particularly well-suited to address several key challenges inherent in language acquisition. One of the most persistent hurdles in learning a foreign language is vocabulary retention—a process often hindered by passive memorization techniques and a lack of meaningful context. Wikis enable students to engage with vocabulary actively, collaboratively building and revising content, which strengthens retention through repeated, purposeful use. Additionally, the interactive nature of wikis helps sustain student engagement, as learners are not merely recipients of information but co-creators of knowledge. This dynamic process encourages deeper cognitive involvement, promoting not only understanding but also application of language skills in authentic contexts.

Importantly, wikis accommodate diverse learning styles, making MFL education more inclusive and motivating. Visual learners benefit from the ability to incorporate images and multimedia, auditory learners can engage with embedded audio content, read/write learners excel through textual contributions, and kinesthetic learners find value in the hands-on editing and collaborative creation process. By offering multiple entry points for engagement, wikis help bridge gaps between different learner preferences, ultimately fostering a richer and more personalized learning experience. This versatility supports differentiated instruction, enabling teachers to tailor activities to meet the needs of a diverse student body.

While the potential benefits of wikis are substantial, challenges remain in effectively integrating this technology into MFL curricula. Technical barriers, uneven student participation, and concerns about linguistic accuracy require careful planning and ongoing support. Moreover, educators need to be equipped with the skills and knowledge to facilitate wiki-based learning, including strategies for scaffolding tasks, monitoring collaboration, and providing timely feedback. Despite these obstacles, the growing body of research and positive case studies suggest that the challenges are surmountable with thoughtful implementation.

Given their promise, wikis deserve continued and focused exploration within MFL settings. Action research, where teachers systematically investigate the impact of wiki use in their own classrooms, combined with consistent student feedback, can provide valuable insights into best practices and areas for improvement. This iterative approach allows educators to refine their methods, ensuring that wikis are not simply an add-on technology but an integral component of effective language teaching. As this chapter has demonstrated, wikis hold the potential to transform MFL classrooms into vibrant hubs of collaboration, creativity, and motivation—key ingredients for successful language learning in today's connected world.

Chapter 5: MFL Theory in the Secondary Sector

Second Language Acquisition (SLA) and foreign language education have been areas of growing interest across the globe (Mitchell & Myles, 2004; Lantolf, 2007; Dixon et al., 2012). However, the study of SLA is not a recent phenomenon; its theoretical foundations have been well-documented over decades (Krashen, 2003). With globalization creating an increased demand for individuals who can communicate in multiple languages, the relevance of language learning has only intensified. The ability to use common languages is particularly crucial in various domains of the social and professional worlds, such as trade, tourism, international relations, technology, media, and science.

Many countries have actively shaped their educational policies to promote foreign language acquisition. For instance, nations such as Korea (Kim Yeong-seo, 2009), Japan (Kubota, 1998), and China (Kirkpatrick & Zhichang, 2002) mandate the teaching of at least one foreign language at both primary and secondary school levels. Meanwhile, countries like India, Singapore, Malaysia, Pakistan, and the Philippines use a second official language in their government systems, further emphasizing the importance of multilingualism.

The term Second Language Acquisition refers to the processes through which individuals acquire one or more additional languages beyond their first language (Nunan, 1999; August & Shanaghan, 2006). Researchers in SLA investigate both naturalistic settings—where learners acquire the language informally through social interaction—and classroom settings. Additionally, SLA research focuses on two major areas: the product of learning (the language acquired) and the process of acquisition (the mental and environmental factors that facilitate learning) (Nunan, 1999; Pinker, 1999; Ellis, 2008).

Purpose and Focus

The primary purpose of this chapter is to explore Second Language Acquisition (SLA) theory comprehensively, with a particular focus on its influence in classroom settings and the learning process itself rather than solely on the product. In agreement with Flint and Peim (2012), the aims are to contribute to improving educational outcomes, including raising standards in education as determined by qualitative metrics of educational performance (Flint & Peim, 2012, pp. 48–49).

Additionally, the chapter seeks to emphasize the importance of learning a second language alongside exploring the most effective methods for doing so. It aims to highlight the influence of existing and contemporary SLA theories on the practical aspects of education, such as teaching strategies, curriculum design, textbooks, policy development, and—most importantly—the learners themselves.

This chapter also highlights the impact of SLA on students and teachers. Students who are a part of the SLA program have reported **cognitive benefits** (enhanced executive function, improved metalinguistic awareness, and increased creativity and divergent thinking), **academic advantages** (superior reading and writing skills, enhanced academic performance, and facilitated learning of additional languages), **neurological benefits** (enhanced brain plasticity, improved neural connectivity, delayed onset of dementia), and finally, **social and cultural benefits** (greater cross-cultural understanding, enhanced communication skills, and broader social networks).

Teachers who are involved in Second Language Acquisition (SLA) instruction have reported professional benefits (enhanced pedagogical skills, increased global employability, and greater job satisfaction), cognitive advantages (improved cognitive flexibility, stronger metalinguistic awareness, and continued language mastery), cultural enrichment (greater intercultural competence, deeper connections with diverse students, and opportunities for cultural exchange), and academic growth (engagement with research-based practices, access to leadership roles, and expanded professional networks).

This chapter also addresses five critical questions for educators, drawing on the foundational work of Nunan (1999) and Krashen (2003):

1. What are the existing Second Language Acquisition theories?
2. How do Second Language Acquisition theories affect teaching?

3. How does information derived from various SLA perspectives influence the formulation of educational MFL policies?
4. How does information derived from SLA theories shape the design of MFL textbooks?
5. What are the implications of SLA theories for second language learners?

The answers to these questions will not only present a comprehensive overview of SLA theories but will also synthesize findings from three key perspectives, which will serve as the foundation for this investigation.

The central hypotheses and frameworks surrounding SLA will be reviewed in this chapter. These theories, which have stood the test of time, remain highly relevant and have also proven useful in other educational contexts. By examining the relevance of SLA theory in the secondary classroom, this chapter supports the perspective of Catherine Ashton, the UK's Parliamentary Under-Secretary of State at the School Standards Office. In her framework for Language for All: A Strategy for England, Ashton emphasizes: "Languages contribute to the cultural and linguistic richness of our society, to personal fulfilment, mutual understanding... we must organize language skills as central to breaking down barriers both within the countries and between nations." (DfES, 2002, p. 4).

Key Perspectives in SLA

1. Contrastive Analysis

Foreign language educators have long utilized linguistic theories through contrastive analysis of the first language (L1) and the second language (L2) for pedagogical purposes. Psycholinguists have continued this practice, analysing where positive or negative transfer may occur for second language learners in different contexts.

2. Sociocultural Hypothesis

The sociocultural hypothesis emphasizes the importance of social interaction in language learning. This perspective has influenced foreign language educators to incorporate more interactive and culturally enriching activities in their classrooms. By examining the cultural dimensions of language learning, this hypothesis has encouraged the integration of authentic materials and real-world communication practices into MFL teaching.

3. Psycholinguistic Perspective

The psycholinguistic perspective focuses on the cognitive processes involved in language learning. While traditionally distinct from sociocultural approaches, psycholinguists have increasingly recognized the importance of sociocultural variables, attempting to integrate these into their frameworks. This perspective examines how learners process linguistic input and how their mental schemas adapt to accommodate new language structures.

Child language researchers, inspired by sociocultural theory, have explored the contexts of second language learning in young learners. However, naturalistic and classroom-based researchers often adopt a psycholinguistic lens when conducting their studies (De Houwer, 2009).

Practical Implications for MFL

1. Policy and Curriculum Design

SLA theories offer valuable insights into the development of educational policies and curricula. For instance, sociocultural theories highlight the need for immersive, interactive language programs that reflect real-world use, while psycholinguistic theories emphasize the importance of scaffolded learning to support cognitive development.

2. Textbook Design

The design of MFL textbooks can also benefit from SLA research. For example, textbooks informed by sociocultural theories may include authentic dialogues, cultural narratives, and collaborative activities, while those drawing on psycholinguistic principles may focus on structured input and graded exercises to facilitate language processing.

Implications for Learners

Ultimately, the goal of SLA research is to improve outcomes for learners. By understanding the cognitive and social processes involved in language acquisition, educators can tailor their teaching methods to better meet the needs of diverse learners.

Second Language Acquisition theory provides a robust framework for understanding how individuals learn additional languages and for improving educational practices in MFL classrooms. By examining the interplay between sociocultural and psycholinguistic perspectives, this chapter highlights the importance of integrating both cognitive and social dimensions into language teaching.

1. **Cognitive Benefits**

Students in the SLA program often report having a higher executive function than their peers. These students often exhibit improved attention, have a higher problem-solving ability than their peers, and show more cognitive flexibility to new concepts. These improved alterations to brain chemistry are often attributed to the brain's management of multiple language models. Each language comes with its own set of rules, stimulating the brain and thereby strengthening the executive control mechanism of these pupils.

This alteration in cognition also allows the child to learn other languages faster. SLA program causes improved metalinguistics awareness, meaning that those children who are fluent in two or more languages develop a heightened understanding of various language structures and functions. This understanding leads to a quicker learning curve for other additional languages, enhancing linguistic skills.

An early exposure to SLA practice can help a child to develop their cognition at a faster rate, fostering creativity and the ability to think divergently. This allows them to approach problems from various perspectives and come with creative solutions, enriching the experience of learning on the classroom.

2. **Academic Advantages**

Students who are a part of the SLA learning program showcase superior reading and writing skills. Since learning a second language can bolster literacy skills in first and second languages, children who are bilingual often show signs of improved reading and writing skills, leading to better reading comprehension and writing abilities.

These children also show signs of enhanced academic performance, often demonstrating higher academic achievements than their peers who are fluent in only one language. This improvement to the academic performance can be attributed to improved cognition and problem-solving abilities. translating into higher scores in subjects such as mathematics and science.

In the classroom, a child who is fluent in multiple languages is very receptive to learn additional languages. Early bilingualism lays a foundation that makes it easy to learn additional languages. This becomes evident when children easily recognize linguistic patterns and structures in different languages, often relating them to their own learned languages, which in turn enhances the learning experience.

3. Neurological Benefits

Bilungilisum not only improves classroom function but also enhances the brain at both anatomical and chemical levels. Learning a second language, particularly during early childhood, increases gray matter density in regions associated with language, memory, and attention. This structural change in the brain is linked to improved neuroplasticity (Mechelli et al., 2004).

Studies have shown visible enhancements in the white matter of the brain, particularly in the corpus callosum (responsible for sharing of information and coordinated communication between the hemispheres) and frontal lobe regions (responsible for higher cognitive functions such as thinking, planning, and problem-solving, along with controlling movement and speech). This promotes seamless communication between brain regions, significantly enhancing executive functions and overall cognitive performance (Luk et al., 2011)

Research also indicates that bilingual people may experience a delayed onset of Alzheimer's disease and other forms of dementia by as much as 4 to 5 years compared to those who speak only one language (Bialystok, Craik, & Freedman, 2007).

4. Social and Cultural Benefits

Bilingual children often experience benefits that range beyond just language skills. One big advantage is the development of a greater appreciation for different cultures, fostering empathy and open-mindedness. As they navigate multiple languages, these children also boost their communication skills, becoming better listeners and more adaptable in various social situations. Furthermore, being bilingual allows them to connect with a diverse group of peers, broadening their social networks and enriching their interactions and experiences. This combination of skills and understanding not only equips them for a more interconnected world but also shapes them into more compassionate and versatile individuals.

5. Long-Term Career Advantages

Command in multiple languages is a valuable asset in the global job market, opening doors to careers in international business, diplomacy, and more. Bilingual individuals often have access to a wider range of educational and professional opportunities, including study abroad programs and international collaborations.

As global interconnectedness continues to grow, the relevance of SLA theory in shaping educational policies, curricula, and classroom practices cannot be overstated. By addressing the challenges of language learning and leveraging insights from SLA research, educators can create more effective, inclusive, and engaging language programs for secondary learners.

Implications for teachers

One of the vital reasons to incorporate Second Language Acquisition (SLA) theory into secondary modern foreign language (MFL) classrooms is its ability to help teachers address the diverse linguistic and cognitive backgrounds of their students. This means shifting away from a one-size-fits-all teaching style and adopting more personalized approaches that consider factors like students' native languages, how old they were when they started learning the language, their previous experience with it, and their individual motivation and anxiety levels.

Imagine a Year 9 student who has always heard Spanish at home but hasn't had any formal lessons. This student will learn and process the language very differently from a classmate who is encountering Spanish for the first time. That's where Second Language Acquisition (SLA) theory becomes helpful. It allows teachers to identify these differences and adjust their teaching strategies to better suit each student's needs.

Teachers can use techniques like targeted support, peer learning, or real-life Spanish materials to enhance understanding. This not only improves language skills but also creates a welcoming classroom atmosphere where every student feels valued, challenged, and supported in their unique learning paths.

By putting SLA theory into practice, we can change the language classroom from a dull space of memorization into an engaging environment that promotes growth and cultural exploration. Students will not only learn a new language; they'll also connect with it on a personal level, making their experience much richer and more enjoyable.

Chapter 6: MFL and Leadership

The role of leadership in education, particularly in Modern Foreign Languages (MFL), is a topic of importance. Effective leadership is increasingly recognized as a critical factor in shaping the success of MFL departments, influencing both teaching practices and student outcomes. This chapter addresses two central questions:

1. How does leadership influence the MFL classroom?
2. Is there a specific type of leadership that benefits the MFL department?

Goals and Objectives

The primary objectives of this chapter are to explore recent developments in MFL education and to examine how effective leadership can drive innovation and improvement in foreign language learning. The focus will be on understanding the evolving trends in MFL instruction over the past decade, emphasizing the importance of leadership styles and management practices in this field.

By addressing these objectives, this chapter highlights the significance of teaching a second language and the relevance of effective leadership in achieving this goal. It also discusses the practical application of leadership theories to improve outcomes in MFL classrooms and departments.

Leadership Influence the MFL Classroom

Leadership plays a critical role in shaping the effectiveness, culture, and outcomes of the Modern Foreign Languages (MFL) classroom. The Harvard Business School defines a manager as someone who "gets results through people" (Templar, 2011, p. 5). Leadership, however, extends beyond management by inspiring, influencing, and guiding individuals toward shared goals. The UK government's White Paper: Success for All (DfES, 2002) emphasized the importance of leadership in education, stating that "developing the leaders, teachers, trainers, and support staff of the future" is central to achieving national educational goals (DfES, 2002, p. 7).

Leadership sets up clear visions and strategic directions for the school to follow. A strong school leadership sets clear visions and pathways for language learning. There are clear expectations from everyone included in the program. Effective leadership that embraces multilingualism can integrate MFL into the wider curriculum. This approach not only enhances the educational experience but also nurtures a culture that appreciates language diversity and promotes global competence.

Ofsted has highlighted that school leaders who devote time to improving professional development in teachers help MFL teachers stay updated on the top practices, and acquire the latest teaching methodologies and advanced digital tools to assist in the enhancement of teaching. By enhancing teacher competence, we also elevate morale, which significantly improves the quality of instruction provided to students.

Transformational leadership plays a key role in fostering innovation in education, especially in the classroom. By encouraging practices like project-based learning, foreign exchange programs, and blending language with cultural insights across various subjects, we can make the Modern Foreign Languages (MFL) classroom a much more engaging and relatable experience for students. This approach not only invigorates learning but also connects with students' lives in meaningful ways (Fullan, 2014).

Leaders who vouch for inclusion in modern foreign language (MFL) classrooms are on the path to creating an environment that welcomes and supports every learner. This actively accommodates students with diverse needs, including those with special educational requirements and those who speak English as a second language. To achieve this, they employ differentiated instruction, tailoring their teaching methods to meet the unique strengths and challenges of each student. Additionally, adaptive assessments are used to evaluate progress in a way that respects each learner's individual journey, ensuring that all students have the opportunity to thrive and succeed in their language studies.

One important but often overlooked role of MFL leaders is to advocate for language learning within the school community. In many schools, foreign languages are pushed aside in favor of STEM subjects or seen as less important for academic success. Effective MFL leaders confront this viewpoint by highlighting the cultural, cognitive, and career advantages of learning a language. They actively engage with school leaders, governors, and parents to share the importance of language studies, ensuring that the subject gets the attention and resources it deserves. By doing this, they help make sure MFL is viewed as an essential part of a well-rounded education, rather than just an optional add-on. This advocacy also boosts the morale of MFL teachers, who often face challenges like staffing cuts or limited class time.

Despite this acknowledgment, Ofsted and other bodies have highlighted persistent weaknesses in leadership and management within the education sector (Clarke, 2004). Lumby (2010) argues for an urgent need to expand the depth and quality of evidence to inform leadership practices and leadership development.

Key Issues in Educational Leadership

Educational leadership is vital in creating high-quality and fair learning environments around the world. Today, as we face rapid changes in technology, shifting social dynamics, and higher expectations for accountability, school leaders are met with a challenging and complex landscape. Their roles are more varied than ever, as they work to promote inclusive education, navigate systemic reforms, support staff well-being, and improve student success. Several critical issues concerning leadership in education must be considered:

Diverse Performance

Individuals perform differently, so leadership development must address implicit theories of leadership and help individuals develop necessary skills (Watson et al., 2002; Lumby, 2010). Each person brings a unique set of experiences, strengths, and challenges to the table, which means that leadership development can't take a one-size-fits-all approach. It's important to understand that everyone has their own beliefs and ideas about what makes a good leader. To truly foster effective leadership, programs must not only acknowledge these different perspectives but also help individuals identify and refine their views on leadership. By doing so, they can build greater self-awareness and confidence in their leadership style. Additionally, providing individuals with the necessary skills is crucial. This could involve training in communication, decision-making, and team building, among other things. By focusing on both personal beliefs and practical skills, we can create more well-rounded leaders who are better equipped to inspire and guide others. Ultimately, effective leadership development is about recognizing and nurturing the diverse potential that exists in each individual.

Fairness and Equity:

Discrimination and unfair practices must be eliminated to ensure equal opportunities and fair outcomes for all (Clarke, 2004). The leaders must recognize and challenge the biases that can influence their decisions and actions. When people face discrimination - whether in the workplace, in education, or in everyday life - it not only affects their individual lives but also undermines the potential of our communities as a whole. By actively working to remove these injustices, we pave the way for a future where everyone, regardless of their background, has the chance to succeed. We must commit to fostering an environment that values diversity and promotes equity, ensuring that all individuals can thrive and contribute their unique talents to society.

Celebrating Differences:

Differences among individuals should be celebrated and used positively to benefit both organizations and individuals (Howes, 2003). When we recognize and value what makes each person unique, we open the door to new ideas and innovative solutions that benefit everyone. In organizations, fostering an inclusive atmosphere where diversity is appreciated can lead to better teamwork, improved creativity, and enhanced problem-solving. When individuals feel respected and valued for who they are, they are more likely to contribute their best work and collaborate effectively with others. This not only aids personal growth but also propels the organization forward. Ultimately, it isn't just about acknowledging that they exist; it's about actively using them to create a brighter, more inclusive future for everyone. By doing so, we can build stronger relationships, drive positive change, and create communities—both in the workplace and beyond—that thrive on diversity and mutual respect.

Work-Life Integration:

Education systems must allow individuals to develop their full potential while respecting personal choices and life circumstances (Lumby, 2010). Education systems play a crucial role in helping individuals unlock their full potential. But for this to happen, they need to have empathy for each person's unique journey. It's important that education respects personal choices and acknowledges life circumstances, whether it's family responsibilities, financial challenges, or different learning styles. When education is tailored to accommodate these factors, it allows everyone to thrive. Imagine a classroom where students feel supported in pursuing their passions, regardless of their background. This kind of environment fosters not only academic success but also personal growth and self-discovery. Ultimately, education should be a journey that empowers individuals to chase their dreams while embracing who they are. By prioritizing respect for personal circumstances, we can create a more inclusive and effective education system that truly benefits everyone.

Positive Psychology in Leadership

Positive psychology offers a revolutionary approach to leadership in education, emphasizing practices that help individuals and organizations achieve their highest potential. Cameron (2013) describes positive leadership as fostering extraordinary performance, vitality, and flourishing within organizations.

Benefits of Positive Psychology in Leadership

1. **Enhanced Performance**: Organizations that implement positive practices tend to experience higher productivity, profitability, and quality, as well as improved customer satisfaction and employee retention (Cameron, 2013).
2. **Individual Well-Being**: Positive leadership impacts individuals' physiological health, emotional well-being, brain functioning, interpersonal relationships, and learning outcomes (Law & Glover, 2000; Balshaw, 2010; Cameron, 2013).
3. **Improved Decision-Making**: Individuals are generally more accurate in processing positive information, which

enhances verbal reasoning, organizational behavior, and emotional judgment (Watkinson, 2003; Cameron, 2013).

Organizational Culture: Positive practices create a culture of collaboration, innovation, and resilience, enabling organizations to thrive even in challenging circumstances (Balshaw, 2010; Cameron, 2013).

However, positive psychology does not imply constant optimism or superficial interactions. Effective leaders must balance positivity with realism, addressing challenges head-on while maintaining a constructive and forward-looking approach.

Leadership in MFL Departments

Leadership in MFL departments plays a unique role in fostering effective teaching and learning. Strong leadership not only influences classroom dynamics but also impacts curriculum development, teacher training, and student motivation.

Influence on the Classroom

Leadership directly affects the quality of instruction in MFL classrooms. Leaders who prioritize collaboration, innovation, and professional development create environments where teachers feel supported and empowered to experiment with new teaching methods. This, in turn, enhances student engagement and learning outcomes.

Leadership Styles Beneficial for MFL

In today's classrooms, especially in the realm of MFL, the impact of emotional intelligence cannot be overstated. Learning a new language isn't just about grammar and vocabulary; it's a deeply personal journey that often brings students face-to-face with vulnerability. They must step outside their comfort zones, embrace risks, and navigate unfamiliar cultural landscapes. This is where leaders with high emotional intelligence play a vital role.

These leaders have a unique ability to sense the emotional atmosphere around them—whether it's in the staff room or the classroom. They know the importance of empathy; they listen when teachers share their struggles, and they notice when a student seems disengaged or anxious. Instead of waiting for problems to arise, emotionally intelligent leaders actively look for signs of burnout among teachers and declining motivation among students. They foster an environment where everyone feels comfortable expressing their concerns and challenges.

By creating psychologically safe spaces, these leaders encourage open dialogue and collaboration. They don't just react to crises but instead anticipate them, empowering their teams to address issues together. This collective approach not only strengthens relationships but also builds resilience within the team.

In MFL environments, where confidence is key and cultural sensitivity is paramount, emotionally intelligent leadership can transform a department. It helps to cultivate a community that embraces inclusivity and trust. When students and staff feel understood and valued, they are more likely to take risks, engage meaningfully in learning, and grow both personally and academically.

Ultimately, it's about more than just teaching a language. It's about nurturing individuals, celebrating diversity, and creating a vibrant dynamic that inspires everyone involved. In this way, emotionally intelligent leaders shape not only successful language learners but also compassionate global citizens.

Certain leadership styles are particularly effective in MFL settings:

1. **Transformational Leadership:** Leaders inspire and motivate their teams by setting a clear vision, fostering creativity, and encouraging professional growth. This style is especially effective in driving innovation in MFL instruction.
2. **Distributed Leadership:** By sharing leadership responsibilities among staff, distributed leadership promotes collaboration and empowers teachers to take initiative in their roles.
3. **Servant Leadership:** Leaders prioritize the needs of their team members, creating a supportive and inclusive environment. This approach is particularly valuable in promoting equity and diversity within MFL departments.

Practical Implications

An important aspect of effective leadership in MFL departments is the integration of mentoring and coaching into team development. Strong leaders recognize that mentoring early career teachers and newly qualified staff is crucial. This support not only deepens their understanding of subject-specific teaching methods but also boosts their confidence and helps them feel more at home in the classroom. When teachers feel supported, they're more likely to stay in the profession, which is essential for maintaining continuity and quality in education. Effective leadership in MFL departments requires the following:

1. **Vision and Strategy**: Leaders must articulate a clear vision for MFL education that aligns with broader school goals.
2. **Professional Development:** Providing training and resources for teachers ensures they stay updated on best practices in language instruction.
3. **Collaboration:** Encouraging teamwork among staff fosters a culture of shared responsibility and innovation.
4. **Student-Centered Practices:** Leadership should prioritize practices that enhance student motivation and engagement in MFL learning.

By promoting a culture of professional dialogue and reflection within the department, MFL leaders create an environment where everyone can grow and learn from one another. This collaborative approach not only strengthens the team but also fosters a sense of belonging and collective purpose. When teachers work together and share their experiences, it builds resilience in the department and leads to improved teaching quality.

Leadership is a critical factor in the success of MFL education. By adopting positive leadership practices and fostering collaboration, MFL departments can overcome challenges and create environments where both teachers and students thrive. The integration of leadership theories into MFL settings offers valuable insights for educators, highlighting the importance of vision, strategy, and inclusivity in driving educational success.

As the education landscape continues to evolve, the role of leadership in MFL will remain central to achieving excellence in language learning. By embracing innovative approaches and fostering a culture of positivity and collaboration, leaders can ensure that MFL departments play a vital role in preparing students for a globalized world.

Chapter 7: Reading a Foreign Language

Reading is often regarded as one of the most critical language skills for students learning a foreign or second language, especially in academic contexts (Grabe, 1991; Huffman, 2014). Despite its central importance, many educational settings around the world continue to rely heavily on traditional methods, such as grammar-translation, which use reading primarily as a tool for grammar and vocabulary acquisition. These methods often neglect the development of fluent reading skills, which are essential for comprehension, enjoyment, and confidence in reading. This chapter explores the role of reading in foreign language learning, emphasizing the need for effective strategies to foster fluency and comprehension.

Although grammar-translation techniques have long been used in language training, their shortcomings are becoming more noticeable in contemporary classrooms. These conventional methods, which rely on translating single sentences and memorizing vocabulary lists, frequently deprive language of its context and intended function. Although they may become proficient at recognizing grammatical structures or translating individual words, students may find it difficult to interact meaningfully with real texts. This misalignment of form and function can make it more difficult for students to naturally assimilate language, turning reading into a robotic activity rather than a chance for discovery and interaction.

A more comprehensive approach to reading, on the other hand, sees it as an active process of meaning-making in which students engage with the text not only to decode but also to understand, consider, and react. Students start internalizing language patterns and gaining the cognitive flexibility necessary to read fluently and comprehendably when they are given the chance to read in a way that corresponds with real-world usage, whether through stories, articles, or dialogues. Because students find the subject personally relevant and enjoyable, this experiential approach not only increases linguistic proficiency but also increases motivation. Reading becomes an experience, a place where language comes to life, rather than a chore.

Furthermore, the advantages of mastering fluent reading in a second language go beyond the confines of the language school. Students improve their critical thinking, cultural sensitivity, and academic resilience as they become more adept at interpreting literature. Effective reading enables students to engage more fully in a globalized world, whether they are reading a news story, following instructions, or reading a literary work. In this sense, encouraging reading fluency is a fundamental investment in a student's overall academic and personal growth rather than just a language acquisition issue.

The Challenge of Developing Fluent Reading Skills

For many learners, the development of strong reading skills requires overcoming a "downward spiral" in which low fluency and comprehension lead to a lack of enjoyment in reading. This lack of enjoyment, in turn, results in reduced practice, which perpetuates low fluency and comprehension (Nuttall, 2005; Stanovich, 2000). This cycle can be particularly detrimental for students learning a foreign language, where additional challenges such as unfamiliar vocabulary, syntax, and cultural context further complicate the reading process.

The emotional toll that this spiral can have is what makes it particularly troublesome for language learners. Frequent encounters with texts that are overpowering, unclear, or difficult to understand can quickly cause annoyance and disinterest. Students start avoiding the activity completely when they absorb the idea that reading in a foreign language is impossible for them, which feeds a vicious cycle that is difficult to stop. When reading is viewed as a competency test rather than a means of communication, the classroom might start to feel more like a place of fear than encouraging. It is equally crucial for educators to identify and solve this emotional barrier as it is to address the cognitive one.

One of the most effective ways to disrupt this cycle is to offer reading experiences that prioritize success and enjoyment early on. Instead of throwing learners into complex texts too soon, educators can provide graded readers, high-interest materials, and scaffolded texts that match students' proficiency levels. When learners experience moments of achievement—understanding a paragraph, following a storyline, or even laughing at a joke in the target language—they begin to reframe their relationship with reading. These small victories accumulate, gradually rebuilding confidence and rekindling curiosity. Over time, reading becomes less about decoding unfamiliar symbols and more about engaging with ideas, characters, and worlds.

Additionally, it's important to recognize that fluency is not built in isolation—it is supported by a broader ecosystem of classroom practices and peer interaction. Group reading tasks, shared storytelling, and discussion-based follow-ups allow students to support each other and process texts collaboratively. Such activities provide a sense of community and shared purpose, helping learners feel less alone in their struggles and more motivated to persist. By embedding reading within a social and supportive framework, educators can create conditions that foster resilience, persistence, and ultimately, a deeper love for the language.

Grabe (2009) observed that teachers are often hesitant to rethink traditional approaches to reading instruction. Many educators and administrators remain uncomfortable with methods that emphasize student autonomy, such as extensive reading, as these approaches may appear to reduce the role of direct teaching. Additionally, there is a perception that increasing reading fluency may not necessarily lead to improved comprehension. To address these concerns, further research is needed to provide empirical evidence of the benefits of fluency-focused reading instruction (Huffman, 2014).

Defining Reading Fluency

Reading fluency refers to the ability to read text rapidly, accurately, and with appropriate expression and prosody (Adams, 1994; Nathan & Stanovich, 1991; Pressley, 2006). However, this definition often assumes that oral reading fluency accurately reflects silent reading fluency, which may not be the case for second-language learners. For these learners, the ability to comprehend text silently may develop independently of the ability to read aloud fluently, as oral reading requires additional skills such as pronunciation and prosody (Lems, 2006; Jeon, 2012).

Extensive Reading: A Path to Fluency

Day and Bamford (1998) outlined the characteristics of extensive reading, an approach to reading instruction designed to promote fluency and comprehension. Key features include:

1. Allowing students to self-select from a wide range of enjoyable reading materials.
2. Ensuring that the reading material is well within the student's ability level.
3. Encouraging students to read extensively but individually.
4. Emphasizing reading speed and enjoyment rather than focusing on grammar and vocabulary acquisition.

Extensive reading has been the subject of significant research over the past three decades, with positive results reported in areas such as incidental vocabulary acquisition (Day, Omura, & Hiramatsu, 1991; Elley, 1991; Mason & Krashen, 1997, 2010; Yag, 2001). Additionally, there is growing evidence that extensive reading can lead to improvements in reading fluency as students develop the ability to read rapidly while maintaining comprehension. However, despite these promising findings, relatively few empirical studies have measured changes in reading rate as an indicator of fluency development (Beglar, Hunt, & Kite, 2012; Grabe, 2009).

The Components of Reading Fluency

There is a consensus among researchers, from Sir Edmund Huey to LaBerge and Samuels (1974) and beyond, that reading fluency involves a set of sub-skills, including:

1. **Decoding**: The ability to translate written symbols into sounds.
2. **Word Recognition**: The ability to identify words rapidly and accurately.
3. **Phonological Representation**: The mental encoding of sounds.
4. **Syntactic and Semantic Parsing**: The ability to group words into meaningful units and understand their relationships.

These sub-skills are gradually automatized through practice, freeing up the reader's cognitive resources for higher-level processes such as comprehension, analysis, and interpretation (Pikulski & Chard, 2005; Wolf & Katzir-Cohen, 2001).

As Wolf and Katzir-Cohen (2001) explain, "If each component process requires attention, the performance of the complex skill will be impossible because the capacity of attention will be exceeded. But if enough of the components and their coordinates can be processed automatically, then the load on attention will be within tolerable limits, and the skill can be successfully performed" (p. 293). Nathan and Stanovich further argue that when word recognition becomes fluent, most of the reader's cognitive capacity can be directed toward higher-level tasks such as analysing and reflecting on the text. Adams (1994) concurs, noting that attention directed toward the mechanics of reading is attention unavailable for comprehension.

This understanding of cognitive load is especially important when working with second-language learners, who are often juggling multiple demands simultaneously. While native speakers may have already automatized basic decoding and word recognition, language learners are still developing those foundational skills while also trying to grasp unfamiliar syntax, idioms, and cultural references. Without sufficient fluency at the word level, their working memory becomes overloaded, making it difficult to construct meaning from the text. This is why seemingly simple tasks—like reading a paragraph or answering comprehension questions—can feel disproportionately exhausting for language learners compared to their native-speaking peers.

Reading education needs to be purposefully scaffolded and sequenced to combat this. Repeated exposure to high-frequency words, organized practice with sentence structures, and activities that prioritize recognition over production are all ways that educators can help students develop automaticity. Students can interact with texts more naturally as these components get more accustomed to them and less cognitively demanding, refocusing their attention from word decoding to meaning construction. True literacy starts to emerge in this area, where reading's mechanical components no longer predominate. Here, students may draw conclusions, recognize tone, and link ideas between paragraphs—skills necessary for both academic achievement and critical interaction with the outside world.

Moreover, fluent reading acts as a gateway to richer language acquisition. When students can process written language smoothly, they are exposed to a broader range of vocabulary, complex grammatical structures, and authentic expressions—all within meaningful contexts. This kind of exposure is difficult to replicate through isolated grammar drills or rote memorization. In essence, fluency does more than make reading easier; it transforms reading into a powerful engine for language growth. Investing in fluency, then, is not just a technical concern—it is a pedagogical priority with far-reaching implications for how students learn, think, and communicate in a new language.

Implications for Foreign Language Instruction

The development of reading fluency in foreign language learners has significant implications for instructional practices. Teachers must prioritize methods that encourage extensive reading, allowing students to encounter language in meaningful and context-rich ways. This approach not only supports vocabulary acquisition and comprehension but also fosters a positive attitude toward reading.

However, implementing extensive reading programs requires careful planning and support. Teachers must ensure that students have access to a wide variety of suitable reading materials and understand the goals of extensive reading. Moreover, professional development and leadership are crucial in helping educators adopt and adapt these methods effectively.

Reading fluency is a cornerstone of foreign language learning, enabling students to access and engage with texts in meaningful ways. Extensive reading offers a powerful tool for developing fluency, comprehension, and confidence, but its implementation requires a shift in mindset for many educators and administrators. By prioritizing fluency and fostering a culture of reading for enjoyment, educators can break the downward spiral of low fluency and comprehension, empowering students to become confident and capable readers in their target language.

This chapter builds on the themes of leadership and innovation explored in previous chapters, emphasizing the importance of adopting evidence-based practices to enhance teaching and learning in Modern Foreign Languages. Through effective leadership and a commitment to student-centred instruction, schools can transform the way reading is taught and learned, ensuring that students not only master the mechanics of reading but also experience the joy and fulfilment that comes with understanding and interpreting texts.

Schools must shift from discrete interventions to a more integrated curriculum design paradigm in order to fully integrate reading fluency into Modern Foreign Languages (MFL) instruction. This means that instead of considering reading as an extra ability, leadership teams must emphasize it as a fundamental component of language development. Important stages include incorporating time for quiet or guided reading into the schedule, creating extensive libraries of level-appropriate books, and integrating structured reading programs. In real life, this could include setting aside certain times each week for reading, incorporating reading into evaluation criteria, or supporting extracurricular activities that call for students to interact with books in the target language.

Professional growth is another crucial element in encouraging reading in MFL. Few language instructors receive professional training in reading pedagogy, particularly in the areas of teaching comprehension and fluency techniques. Instruction may therefore fall back on more conventional techniques like translation or text-based grammar exercises. Schools should spend money on training that gives instructors evidence-based methods for promoting reading fluency in order to change this. Workshops may concentrate on methods such as vocabulary pre-teaching, guided reading groups, post-reading discussions, and pre-reading schema activation. Collaborative sessions when they exchange achievements, difficulties, and useful ideas for creating a classroom climate that is rich in reading can be beneficial to even seasoned language teachers.

Teacher beliefs also play a significant role in shaping classroom practice. If educators perceive reading in the target language as too advanced for their students, or worry that fluency takes too long to develop, they may unintentionally lower expectations or avoid reading altogether. Changing these mindsets requires more than just training—it involves cultivating a professional culture that values reading as a long-term investment. School leaders can support this by recognizing and celebrating growth in reading fluency, even when gains are gradual. When teachers see that their efforts are producing real progress, they are more likely to persist and innovate in their approaches.

Family engagement is another often overlooked but powerful lever for supporting reading in MFL. While most parents may not speak the language their children are learning, they can still encourage positive reading habits. Providing families with strategies for supporting reading at home—such as creating quiet reading spaces, celebrating completed books, or encouraging storytelling in any language—helps bridge school and home learning environments. Schools might also consider sending home bilingual books, creating family reading logs, or holding MFL-themed reading challenges. These efforts help demystify the process of language learning and position reading as a communal rather than isolated experience.

In the current digital environment, technology offers reading teachers both advantages and disadvantages. On the one hand, students now have unparalleled access to a variety of digital materials in the target language, including blogs, short stories, news items, and even posts on social media. However, there are many distractions and reading online frequently promotes skimming rather than in-depth reading. As a result, educators need to use digital resources deliberately. E-readers with built-in dictionaries, platforms that monitor reading progress, or carefully curated digital reading lists are a few examples of tools that might improve motivation and offer customized assistance. With careful integration, technology can act as a scaffold rather than a shortcut, enabling children to read more extensively and with greater assurance.

Assessment practices should also reflect a deeper understanding of reading fluency. Traditional assessments tend to focus on discrete comprehension questions or translation tasks that do not capture the richness of a student's reading ability. Alternative assessments—such as reading journals, fluency recordings, summaries in the target language, or peer-led book talks—offer more authentic glimpses into student progress. These tools also promote metacognitive awareness, as learners begin to monitor their own understanding, identify unfamiliar words, and reflect on their growth over time. Teachers who use these methods not only assess better but also teach students how to become more strategic and independent readers.

Importantly, the value of reading extends beyond its utility as a language skill. When students read in another language, they encounter new cultures, perspectives, and worldviews. A well-chosen text can spark empathy, curiosity, and a deeper understanding of global issues. Whether through a personal narrative set in Latin America, a poem from the Francophone world, or an article about youth activism in Germany, reading allows students to see the world through someone else's eyes. These experiences are not just academically enriching—they are humanizing. They build intercultural competence, a core goal of modern language education.

At the same time, reading should also allow students to see themselves reflected in what they read. For example, offering texts that feature multilingual or immigrant protagonists, stories of language learning journeys, or narratives that connect to students' lived experiences can create powerful moments of recognition. These stories affirm identity and provide encouragement to learners who may be navigating complex relationships with language, belonging, or confidence. In this way, inclusive reading materials do more than support fluency—they build classroom communities where every student feels seen, valued, and empowered.

Furthermore, reading offers opportunities for interdisciplinary collaboration. Language teachers can work with colleagues in history, geography, literature, or citizenship to select texts that complement wider curricular goals. For instance, reading a diary from a young refugee in Spanish can tie into discussions about migration and human rights, while exploring a French environmental article can enrich debates in science or global studies. These interdisciplinary links not only make reading more meaningful but also help students understand that language is not confined to a subject—it is a tool for navigating the world.

Ultimately, the journey toward fluent and joyful reading in a foreign language is not a linear one. There will be moments of struggle, setbacks, and resistance—both from learners and educators. But when schools commit to this goal with intention, creativity, and compassion, the rewards are profound. Reading becomes more than an academic skill; it becomes a doorway to connection, expression, and lifelong learning. Students begin to see language not as a barrier but as a bridge—one that leads to new stories, new people, and new possibilities.

In conclusion, enhancing reading in Modern Foreign Languages requires a multifaceted, whole-school approach. From curriculum design and teacher training to family engagement and technology integration, every layer of the school ecosystem plays a role. Evidence-based practices, when applied with care and contextual understanding, can dramatically improve not only how students read, but how they feel about reading. When we give learners the tools, time, and trust to read deeply and often, we prepare them not just to succeed in exams, but to thrive in a multilingual, multicultural world. Through reading, we don't just teach language—we open windows to understanding, empathy, and empowerment.

Chapter 8: Differentiation in Modern Education

In the 21st-century classroom, diversity is not just a demographic reality—it is the defining feature of the learning environment. Students arrive with different languages, learning histories, cognitive profiles, emotional needs, and cultural identities. While this diversity enriches the educational experience, it also presents complex challenges for educators tasked with meeting the needs of all learners. Traditional, one-size-fits-all teaching approaches, which may have once sufficed in more homogeneous settings, are increasingly inadequate. The evolving nature of education demands pedagogies that are flexible, inclusive, and responsive to individual differences. Within this landscape, differentiation emerges not as an optional enhancement but as a foundational approach to equity and effectiveness in teaching.

More than just a response to academic variation, differentiation addresses the full spectrum of learner variability—encompassing motivation, self-regulation, learning pace, and socio-emotional development. It aligns closely with the broader educational goals of personalized learning and inclusive practice, offering a framework that honours the dignity and potential of each student. At its heart, differentiation is about anticipating and planning for difference, rather than reacting to it after the fact. This proactive mindset shifts the teacher's role from content deliverer to learning architect—someone who designs multiple entry points and pathways through which every student can thrive. It is within this context that the following discussion unfolds.

Differentiation remains an essential cornerstone of effective teaching in today's diverse classrooms. As Carol Ann Tomlinson, a leading authority on differentiated instruction, emphasizes, the practice of differentiation is about placing students at the centre of the learning process and giving them ownership of their learning journey. It is not merely a teaching strategy but a philosophy of compassion and inclusivity that recognizes the unique strengths, needs, and challenges of every learner.

Tomlinson, author of The Differentiated Classroom: Responding to the Needs of All Learners, highlights that differentiation is not about lowering standards or diminishing rigor.

Instead, it is about creating pathways for all students to experience success, even if those pathways look different for each learner. Differentiation lifts students up by meeting them where they are, fostering growth, and challenging them appropriately.

One of the most persistent misconceptions surrounding differentiation is the assumption that it simply means assigning easier work to struggling students. In truth, differentiation is not about diluting the curriculum; rather, it is about refining the approach so that every learner can access, engage with, and master the content. It involves varying the **process**, **product**, **content**, or **learning environment** according to students' readiness, interests, and learning profiles. For instance, a student with strong verbal reasoning but lower reading fluency might express understanding through an oral presentation rather than a written essay. At its best, differentiation creates a sense of intellectual stretch for all students, ensuring that high-achieving pupils are challenged while those who need support are scaffolded effectively—not simplified for, but supported to thrive.

This chapter builds on the themes of leadership, motivation, and collaborative teaching explored in earlier chapters and introduces differentiation as a compassionate practice that addresses the holistic needs of learners. Differentiation is not just about curriculum design or instructional strategies—it is deeply tied to the teacher-student relationship, the teacher's mindset, and the classroom environment.

A key driver of effective differentiation is the thoughtful use of formative assessment. Teachers who embed regular, low-stakes checks for understanding—such as exit tickets, think-pair-share discussions, or quick quizzes—gain valuable insights into students' current grasp of the material. This information empowers them to adjust instruction in real time, whether by regrouping learners, offering additional modelling, or extending a task for those ready to move ahead. Importantly, formative assessment goes beyond collecting data; it invites a dialogue between student and teacher. When learners are encouraged to reflect on their own progress, set goals, and understand their next steps, they become active participants in their own learning. This collaborative approach aligns directly with the heart of differentiation: responsive, student-centred teaching that adapts to real needs, not just perceived ones.

The Principles of Differentiation

Differentiation is guided by several core principles that align with the broader goals of education: Student-Centred Learning: Differentiation prioritizes the student over subject content. Teachers must understand their students as individuals—knowing their strengths, interests, and areas of need. This requires building strong teacher-student connections and creating an environment where all learners feel supported.

Understanding students as individuals also means recognizing that learning is not a linear journey, and progress may look different for each learner. Some students may need more time to process information or may benefit from revisiting content through multiple formats—such as visuals, discussions, or hands-on tasks—before they fully grasp it. Others may thrive when given opportunities to delve deeper into a topic or explore real-world applications. Differentiation allows for this kind of flexibility by encouraging teachers to provide varied levels of support, challenge, and choice. When learners feel seen and understood in these ways, they are more likely to take intellectual risks, engage meaningfully, and persist through difficulties.

Moreover, student-centred differentiation fosters a culture of respect and mutual responsibility within the classroom. When students observe that their peers are receiving different types of support or assignments, clear communication about the purpose of differentiation helps prevent misconceptions or feelings of unfairness. Teachers who model openness and invite students to take part in shaping their learning pathways empower them to advocate for their own needs. This not only strengthens students' academic agency but also prepares them for collaborative environments beyond school, where diverse abilities and working styles are the norm. Ultimately, differentiation grounded in student-centred values contributes to a more just, responsive, and empowering learning environment for all.

1. **Growth Mindset**: Teachers must adopt a growth mindset, believing in the potential of every student to improve and succeed. This mindset encourages teachers to view challenges as opportunities for growth rather than barriers.

2. **Formative Assessment**: Regular formative assessments help teachers understand where students are in relation to the curriculum. This data enables teachers to adjust their instruction to meet students' needs effectively.
3. **Flexibility and Adaptability**: Differentiation requires teachers to be flexible leaders, capable of adjusting their plans, strategies, and expectations based on the dynamic needs of their students.
4. **Compassionate Practice**: Differentiation is an act of compassion that involves understanding and responding to the emotional and academic needs of students. This includes practicing self-compassion as a teacher, and recognizing that one cannot pour from an empty cup.

Compassion in Differentiation

Compassion is often an overlooked yet critical component of effective differentiation. While it can be easier to show compassion toward enthusiastic and well-behaved students, the real challenge lies in extending compassion to "difficult" students—those who may test the teacher's patience or disrupt the learning environment. However, these students often provide the greatest opportunities for teachers to deepen their practice of differentiation.

Compassionate differentiation requires teachers to:

1. Recognize that all students, even those who are challenging, want to be happy and free from suffering.
2. Avoid negative judgments and criticisms, which only create barriers between teacher and student.
3. Practice self-compassion, understanding that teachers, too, need care and support to remain effective and motivated.

Christopher K. Germer, in his book The Mindful Path to Self-Compassion, outlines four healing elements of compassion: intention, attention, emotion, and connection. These elements are deeply relevant to differentiation:

1. **Intention**: Teachers must approach differentiation with the intention of supporting every student's growth and well-being.
2. **Attention**: Teachers need to pay close attention to individual student needs, strengths, and progress.

3. **Emotion**: Differentiation should foster positive emotions, such as confidence and joy, in both students and teachers.
4. **Connection**: Building meaningful connections between teacher and student creates a classroom environment where students feel valued and understood.

Practical Strategies for Differentiation

Differentiation does not need to be overly complicated or burdensome. However, it does require effort, reflection, and a willingness to move beyond traditional teaching habits. The following strategies can help teachers implement differentiation effectively:

Plan for the ablest, scaffold for others: Begin lesson planning with high expectations for the ablest students, then scaffold learning to ensure all students can access the content. This approach maintains rigor while providing necessary support.

1. **Self-Selection and Choice**: Offer students opportunities to choose activities or materials that align with their interests and abilities. This fosters ownership and motivation.
2. **Flexible Grouping**: Use flexible grouping strategies to allow students to work with peers who share similar needs, interests, or abilities. Groups can be dynamic and change based on the task or learning objective.
3. **Varied Instructional Methods**: Incorporate a variety of teaching methods, such as visual aids, hands-on activities, and collaborative projects, to address different learning styles and preferences.
4. **Ongoing Assessment**: Use formative assessments to gather data on student progress and adjust instruction as needed.
5. **Focus on Strengths**: Recognize and build on each student's strengths while addressing areas of need in a supportive manner.
6. **Encourage Reflection**: Create opportunities for students to reflect on their learning and set personal goals.

The Impact of Differentiation

When differentiation is practiced with intention and compassion, it can transform the classroom into a vibrant, inclusive community where all students feel valued and supported. Differentiation fosters:

1. **Positive Relationships**: Compassionate differentiation strengthens the teacher-student bond, creating a sense of trust and mutual respect.
2. **Confidence and Motivation**: Students develop confidence in their abilities and are motivated to take ownership of their learning.
3. **A Sense of Belonging**: Differentiation helps create a classroom environment where diversity is celebrated and every student feels they belong.
4. **Lifelong Learning Skills**: By addressing individual needs and promoting autonomy, differentiation equips students with the skills they need to succeed beyond the classroom.

In conclusion, differentiation is more than an instructional strategy—it is a philosophy grounded in compassion, equity, and inclusivity. By prioritizing the needs of students and fostering a growth-oriented, supportive environment, teachers can help all learners achieve their potential. As Carol Ann Tomlinson reminds us, differentiation is an act of compassion, requiring teachers to be flexible, self-aware, and committed to their students' success. In the broader context of education, differentiation aligns with the principles of leadership, motivation, and collaborative learning explored in previous chapters. It challenges us to rethink traditional practices and embrace a more student-centred approach to teaching, one that recognizes the unique strengths and needs of every learner. Through differentiation, we not only support academic growth but also nurture the emotional and social well-being of our students, preparing them for success in an increasingly diverse and interconnected world.

As schools continue to navigate the demands of a changing educational landscape, the importance of differentiation will only grow. With the rise of inclusive education, neurodiversity awareness, and mental health considerations in schools, the traditional model of uniform instruction is no longer sufficient. Differentiation empowers teachers to honour the full spectrum of learner identities—not just in ability, but in experience, language, background, and belief. This means moving beyond surface-level adjustments to engage in truly responsive pedagogy: one that listens, adapts, and evolves in step with the learners it serves. When differentiation becomes embedded in a school's culture, it signals a broader commitment to educational justice and learner dignity.

At a systemic level, supporting differentiation requires more than just goodwill—it calls for structural and institutional backing. Leaders must ensure that teachers have the time, resources, and professional development needed to implement differentiated practices with confidence and consistency. This includes access to collaborative planning time, relevant training in inclusive methodologies, and opportunities to share best practices across departments. Moreover, assessment policies and curriculum frameworks must allow room for flexibility, acknowledging that success does not always look the same for every student. When differentiation is supported from the top down and the bottom up, it becomes a sustainable force for transformation in teaching and learning.

Ultimately, differentiation invites us to reimagine the purpose of education itself—not as a system designed to sort and rank, but as a space for every learner to flourish. It shifts the teacher's role from delivering content to cultivating potential, from managing behaviour to fostering belonging. This transformation does not happen overnight, nor does it come without challenges. But when educators commit to differentiation with intention, integrity, and care, they create classrooms where every student feels seen, heard, and empowered. And in doing so, they lay the foundation for not just better academic outcomes, but more compassionate, inclusive communities—both within and beyond the school walls.

Chapter 9: Expertise in Teaching

Expertise in teaching is a concept that has gained significant attention in recent years, yet it remains an area that is often generalized and not as deeply explored as it should be in the field of education. Researchers such as David Berliner, John Hattie, and more recently, Ericsson and Pool have contributed substantially to the broader understanding of expertise, including its application in teaching. Berliner's seminal work in Describing the Behaviour and Documenting the Accomplishment of Expert Teachers (2004) and Hattie's extensive research on visible learning have laid the groundwork for analysing what makes expert teachers stand out. Ericsson and Pool, in their book Peak: Secrets from the New Science of Expertise (2016), provide further insights into the science of expertise, though their work is not teacher specific.

Building on these foundational studies, Lorna Shires, a principal lecturer in initial teacher education and researcher at Oxford Brookes University, has contributed to narrowing the focus to teacher expertise. Shires defines teacher expertise as the ability to bridge the gap between students and the subject content, fostering meaningful connections and positive experiences. This chapter will explore the nature of teacher expertise, its unique relational aspects, and its impact on both teaching and learning.

The Nature of Teacher Expertise

Teacher expertise goes beyond mastery of subject knowledge. While having a deep understanding of the subject is essential, expert teachers also possess relational expertise— a unique ability to connect with students and guide them in engaging with the subject matter. According to Shires, expert teachers plan their lessons to help students not only understand key concepts but also apply them in meaningful ways. They present foundational ideas first, revisit these ideas to reinforce understanding, and gradually layer in details and precision over time.

A defining characteristic of teacher expertise is the ability to inspire students to love the subject. Passion for a subject is contagious; when a teacher is deeply in love with what they teach, students are more likely to develop a similar affection. Mihaly Csikszentmihalyi

(2014) described this as entering a state of flow—a condition of complete immersion and joy in an activity that contributes to human well-being. Teachers who are passionate about their subjects bring not just cognitive understanding but emotional depth to their teaching, enabling students to engage with learning on multiple levels.

However, teaching expertise is not just about passion or cognitive competence; it also involves emotional intelligence and a profound sense of compassion. Expert teachers demonstrate kindness and understanding toward themselves, their students, and the subject they teach. They do not strive for perfectionism, which can lead to self-criticism and feelings of inadequacy. Instead, they exhibit a balanced behaviour characterized by concentration, attention, and forgiveness when mistakes occur.

Compassion and Expertise

Compassion is a critical component of teacher expertise. Expert teachers recognize that teaching is not a linear process and that disturbances—whether in the classroom environment, the learning process, or individual students—are inevitable. Rather than resisting or driving out these challenges, expert teachers embrace them with compassion. They integrate disruptions into the learning process, creating opportunities for growth and transformation.

Adapting to the diverse learning needs of students is a critical component of teacher expertise. In any classroom, students come with varying levels of background knowledge, learning styles, and personal experiences that influence their approach to learning. Expert teachers are able to recognize these differences and adjust their teaching strategies to ensure that every student has the opportunity to succeed. This might include differentiating instruction, providing various modes of representation (visual, auditory, kinesthetic), or offering alternative assessment methods. Furthermore, expert teachers are attuned to students' emotional and social needs, understanding that these factors can significantly impact learning. By creating a classroom environment where all students feel valued and supported, expert teachers ensure that their teaching is inclusive and responsive to the individual needs of each learner.

Compassionate teachers exhibit the following behaviours:

1. **Attention to Detail:** Expert teachers' pay close attention to the nuances of their students, the subject, and the teaching process. They notice what is happening in the moment without judgment, allowing them to respond thoughtfully and effectively.
2. **Emotional Intelligence:** They remain emotionally present, understanding their own emotions and those of their students. This emotional intelligence enables them to create a supportive and nurturing learning environment.

Collaboration among teachers plays a pivotal role in the development of expertise. Expert teachers recognize that they are not isolated in their practice but are part of a larger educational community. Engaging in collaborative activities such as team teaching, co-planning lessons, or participating in professional learning communities allows teachers to share strategies, ideas, and resources that can enhance their practice. This collaborative spirit promotes an exchange of diverse perspectives, which is crucial for refining teaching techniques and broadening the scope of one's pedagogical toolbox. Expert teachers also seek feedback from colleagues, embracing a growth mindset that encourages openness to constructive criticism. By working together, teachers can not only improve their individual teaching practices but also contribute to a broader culture of excellence within their school or district.

1. **Integration of Challenges:** When challenges arise, expert teachers address them with kindness and understanding. They welcome disruptions as opportunities to expand knowledge and deepen the learning experience.
2. **Fostering Connection:** By building meaningful relationships with their students, expert teachers create a sense of community in the classroom. This connection helps students feel valued, supported, and more open to learning.

The role of compassion in expertise aligns closely with the themes of differentiation explored in the previous chapter. Both differentiation and expertise require teachers to understand their students as individuals and to respond to their unique needs with empathy and flexibility.

Expertise vs. Perfectionism

It is important to distinguish between expertise and perfectionism. While expert teachers strive for high teaching standards, they do so with a sense of balance and realism. Perfectionists, on the other hand, often set unattainable goals for themselves and experience constant self-criticism when they fall short. This mindset can lead to burnout and a negative classroom environment.

Expert teachers, in contrast, view mistakes as opportunities for growth—for themselves and their students. They approach teaching with a spirit of curiosity and openness, recognizing that the learning process is dynamic and ever-evolving. By modeling this mindset, they encourage their students to take risks, embrace challenges, and develop resilience.

The Impact of Expertise on the Classroom

The presence of an expert teacher transforms the classroom into a space of intellectual and emotional growth. Expert teachers elevate their students by:

1. Creating an atmosphere of trust and respect, where students feel safe to express their ideas and take risks.
2. Helping students connect academic content to their own lives, making learning relevant and meaningful.
3. Encouraging students to think critically and creatively, fostering a deeper understanding of the subject.
4. Supporting students' emotional well-being, helping them develop confidence and a positive attitude toward learning.

Expert teachers also elevate themselves by continually reflecting on their practice, seeking feedback, and pursuing professional growth.

A critical but often overlooked aspect of teaching expertise is the well-being of the teacher. The demanding nature of teaching—dealing with diverse student needs, navigating administrative responsibilities, and maintaining engagement in the classroom—can lead to burnout if not carefully managed. Expert teachers understand the importance of maintaining a healthy work-life balance, engaging in self-care practices, and seeking professional support when necessary. They also recognize that their own emotional and physical well-being directly impacts their effectiveness in the classroom. By prioritizing their mental and emotional health, teachers are better equipped to sustain the energy, creativity, and empathy needed for their roles. Supporting teachers' well-being is essential for ensuring long-term success in the profession, and schools must provide the necessary resources and structures to support their staff's health and wellness.

They understand that expertise is not a fixed state but a lifelong journey of learning and improvement.

An essential aspect of teacher expertise is **reflective practice**, the ongoing process by which teachers critically examine their own teaching. This reflection not only enables teachers to identify areas for growth but also fosters a deeper understanding of their instructional strategies and their effectiveness. Expert teachers engage in reflection both formally and informally. Formal reflection might involve regularly assessing student performance through formative assessments or peer evaluations, while informal reflection can happen through daily journaling or casual self-evaluations. This continual process of introspection allows expert teachers to adjust their teaching approach, ensuring that their methods remain responsive to the changing needs of their students. Furthermore, reflective practice encourages teachers to challenge their assumptions and biases, leading to more inclusive and adaptive teaching styles.

Teacher expertise is a powerful force in education, shaping not only what students learn but how they learn and who they become. It is a dynamic interplay of subject knowledge, relational skills, emotional intelligence, and compassion. Expert teachers inspire their students to love learning, embrace challenges, and strive for excellence.

In the modern educational landscape, technology integration has become a key facet of teaching expertise. Expert teachers not only leverage technology to enhance student learning but also use it to engage students in creative, dynamic, and personalized ways. Digital tools can serve as platforms for collaboration, communication, and interactive learning, enabling students to access resources and participate in activities beyond the traditional classroom setting. Whether it's through online simulations, educational apps, or virtual discussions, technology can deepen students' understanding of content and foster a more inclusive learning environment. However, technology integration must be purposeful and intentional; it is not about simply adding devices or software to the classroom but about using these tools to achieve specific educational goals. Expert teachers are adept at balancing the use of technology with traditional teaching methods, ensuring that it complements rather than detracts from the core learning experience.

As this chapter highlights, expertise in teaching is not about perfection but about presence—being fully engaged with the students, the subject, and the process of learning. By integrating compassion, passion, and expertise, teachers can create transformative educational experiences that leave a lasting impact on their students and themselves.

Chapter 10: Teaching, Learning, and Leading through Covid-19

The Covid-19 pandemic has been one of the most significant global challenges of the 21st century, profoundly impacting every aspect of life, including education. Since December 2019, when the virus first emerged, the world has grappled with unprecedented uncertainty, loss, and change. In the UK alone, 4.4 million confirmed cases and more than 127,000 deaths have been recorded. The rapid rollout of vaccines has provided hope, with over 50 million doses administered and significant reductions in hospitalizations and fatalities. However, the pandemic's impact on education has been far-reaching, affecting teachers, students, and leaders alike in ways that continue to unfold.

This chapter explores the realities of teaching, learning, and leadership during the Covid-19 pandemic. It reflects on the challenges, adaptations, and lessons learned, emphasizing the importance of compassion, resilience, and connection in navigating this evolving landscape. Building on themes of differentiation, expertise, and relational teaching explored in earlier chapters, this chapter highlights how educators can support one another and their students during these turbulent times.

The Challenges of Teaching during a Pandemic

Teaching during a pandemic has presented a unique set of challenges. Social distancing, mask mandates, and the constant threat of infection have disrupted traditional teaching practices. Teachers have had to adapt to online teaching, hybrid models, and ever-changing policies, all while managing their own anxieties and uncertainties.

The sudden shift to remote learning during the pandemic has had far-reaching effects that will likely influence education for years to come. While the transition to virtual classrooms was necessary in the face of the pandemic, it exposed significant disparities in access to technology and digital literacy. Many students, particularly from disadvantaged backgrounds, struggled with a lack of reliable internet access and appropriate devices. As a result, educators had to innovate, often relying on phone calls, printed materials, or creative solutions to bridge the digital divide. This experience highlighted the need for greater investment in digital infrastructure and teacher training to ensure that all students, regardless of their socio-economic status, have equal opportunities to succeed in an increasingly digital world. While remote learning may have been a temporary measure, its long-term effects will continue to reshape the landscape of education, pushing institutions toward more inclusive and tech-savvy models of teaching and learning.

Additionally, the emotional toll on educators has been significant. Many have faced worries of testing positive, concerns about their students' well-being, and pressures of maintaining academic progress in an unpredictable environment. The shift to remote learning has also required teachers to develop new skills and strategies, often with little training or support.

The pandemic spurred an unprecedented wave of innovation in teaching methods. As traditional in-person lessons transitioned to online formats, educators quickly adopted and experimented with new tools, resources, and teaching strategies. Platforms like Zoom, Google Classroom, and Microsoft Teams became indispensable for maintaining continuity in education. In addition to technical tools, teachers embraced more interactive and engaging teaching methods, such as flipped classrooms, gamification, and virtual breakout rooms, which not only kept students engaged but also fostered a sense of community despite the physical separation. Some teachers even began incorporating mindfulness exercises or virtual field trips to help students feel connected to the world outside their homes. These innovations have forever altered the landscape of education, offering teachers and students a broader spectrum of possibilities for personalized and creative learning.

Despite these challenges, teaching remains a deeply rewarding profession. Teachers continue to make a difference in their students' lives, offering stability, inspiration, and guidance in a time of upheaval. As one educator reflects, "I feel teachers can really make a difference in the lives of others. Despite the challenges, teaching still inspires me with admiration and respect."

Leadership during Covid-19

The pandemic has also tested educational leaders, from heads of departments to school principals. Leaders have had to make rapid decisions, implement government guidelines, and address the concerns of staff, parents, and students. The media's scrutiny of school leaders has added another layer of pressure, as has the need to maintain morale among staff who may feel pessimistic or overwhelmed.

Effective leadership during Covid-19 has required adaptability, empathy, and a commitment to collaboration. Leaders who prioritize the well-being of their staff and students, communicate transparently, and model resilience have been better equipped to navigate the challenges of the pandemic.

The challenges presented by the Covid-19 pandemic have catalyzed a shift in leadership styles within the education sector. In times of crisis, the ability of leaders to demonstrate calm, empathy, and decisiveness becomes paramount. Principals and department heads have had to lead by example, showing vulnerability while also providing clarity in a rapidly changing environment. The pandemic has underscored the importance of **transformational leadership**, where leaders not only manage logistics but also inspire and support their teams through periods of uncertainty. It has also highlighted the value of **distributed leadership**, where decision-making is shared, empowering teachers and staff to take initiative in problem-solving. As educational leaders reflect on their pandemic experiences, there will likely be a lasting emphasis on collaboration, adaptability, and the prioritization of emotional intelligence in leadership training and development.

The Student Experience

For students, the pandemic has brought its own set of difficulties. School closures, online learning, and social isolation have disrupted their routines and impacted their mental health. Many students have struggled with motivation, concentration, and feelings of loneliness. For college students (ages 16-19), this period of life—already marked by significant physical, emotional, and social changes—has been particularly challenging.

Yet, despite these obstacles, students have shown remarkable adaptability. They have embraced new ways of learning, developed digital skills, and found creative ways to stay connected with their peers. Teachers have played a crucial role in supporting students through this period, offering not only academic instruction but also emotional support and companionship.

Compassionate Teaching in Times of Crisis

Compassionate teaching has been a lifeline for many students during the pandemic. By being present, empathetic, and accepting, teachers have provided a sense of stability and security in uncertain times. As one teacher reflects:

"Since Covid-19 appeared in our lives, I have felt the need to be present for my students— open and accepting to what they showed me and felt. I may not be able to fix their uncertainties, but by being there with them, I know I have helped them to feel accepted and helped them make sense of things."

This kind of compassionate, attuned teaching creates a safe space for students to process their emotions, adapt to new challenges, and find meaning in their experiences. It also fosters a sense of connection and community, helping students feel less alone during these difficult times.

Lessons Learned

The Covid-19 pandemic has underscored the importance of adaptability, empathy, and resilience in education. It has also highlighted the value of human connection, both within and beyond the classroom. Key lessons for educators and leaders include:

1. **Flexibility is Essential**: The pandemic has shown that educators must be prepared to adapt to changing circumstances, whether through online teaching, hybrid models, or new health and safety protocols.
2. **Compassionate Leadership Matters**: Effective leaders prioritize the well-being of their staff and students, fostering a culture of support and collaboration.

3. **Connection is Key**: Building strong relationships with students, colleagues, and parents is more important than ever. These connections provide a foundation of trust and support that helps everyone navigate challenges together.
4. **Mental Health is a Priority**: The pandemic has brought mental health to the forefront of education. Schools must continue to prioritize the emotional well-being of students and staff, providing resources and support as needed.
5. **The Role of Technology**: While online learning cannot replace in-person interaction, it has become an integral part of education. Teachers and leaders must continue to develop their digital skills and explore innovative ways to engage students online.
6. **Moving Forward**: As the world begins to recover from the pandemic, education faces a critical moment of reflection and transformation. The challenges of Covid-19 have exposed weaknesses in traditional systems but have also created opportunities for growth and innovation. Educators, leaders, and students have demonstrated remarkable resilience, and their experiences during this time will shape the future of teaching and learning.

The Covid-19 pandemic has magnified existing inequalities in education, from disparities in access to technology to the uneven quality of remote learning experiences. As we move into the post-pandemic era, there is a critical need for systemic change that addresses these inequities. Schools and policymakers must prioritize **equitable access to resources**, ensuring that all students, regardless of their background, have the tools they need to succeed in an increasingly digital world. This might include investments in broadband infrastructure, providing devices for students, and offering tailored support for students with disabilities or those from low-income families. Moreover, the pandemic has underscored the importance of creating **inclusive learning environments** that support diverse needs, where every student can thrive. By addressing these equity gaps head-on, the education system can emerge stronger and more capable of providing meaningful learning experiences for all students.

Ultimately, the pandemic has reminded us of the profound impact that compassionate, relational teaching can have on students' lives. By prioritizing connection, empathy, and adaptability, educators can continue to inspire and support their students, no matter the challenges they face.

In the words of an educator, "Being a compassionate teacher, and having an empathetic approach toward my students, has contributed to my students' sense of security. In these difficult times, I have learned that even the smallest acts of kindness and understanding can make all the difference."

Chapter 11: The Power of Mindset in Education

Mindset plays a pivotal role in shaping the outcomes of teaching and learning. Carol Susan Dweck, one of the world's leading researchers in the fields of personality, social, and developmental psychology, has significantly contributed to our understanding of how beliefs about intelligence influence motivation, resilience, and achievement. Dweck's work on mindsets—the concepts of fixed and growth mindsets—has transformed educational practices across the globe and continues to inspire educators to foster a culture of learning, effort, and growth in their classrooms.

This chapter explores the concept of mindset, its implications for teaching and learning, and how educators can integrate a growth mindset approach into their practices. Building on previous chapters that emphasized differentiation, expertise, and compassionate teaching, this chapter highlights the transformative power of mindset in creating positive educational environments where all learners can thrive.

Understanding Fixed and Growth Mindsets

Carol Dweck (2006) developed the concept of mindset from two perspectives: the fixed mindset and the growth mindset. These perspectives describe how individuals perceive their own abilities, particularly intelligence:

1. **Growth Mindset:** Individuals with a growth mindset believe that intelligence is not fixed but can be developed through effort, learning, and persistence. They embrace challenges, view failures as opportunities to grow, and are more likely to bounce back after setbacks.
2. **Fixed Mindset:** Individuals with a fixed mindset believe that intelligence is a stable, unchangeable trait. They tend to avoid challenges, fear failure as a reflection of their abilities, and feel helpless when they encounter obstacles.

Dweck's research revealed that students who adopt a growth mindset outperform those with a fixed mindset. Furthermore, interventions that teach students to believe in their ability to "grow their brains" and increase their intellectual capacities have shown to improve academic outcomes (Dweck, 2015). The simplicity and intuitive nature of this idea have made it widely accepted among educators, as it resonates with the belief that everyone has the potential to grow and succeed.

One of the most important applications of a growth mindset is in teaching students how to overcome setbacks. Failure, while difficult, is an essential part of the learning process, and students with a growth mindset are more resilient in the face of adversity. When students view challenges as opportunities to grow, they are more likely to persist, even when they struggle. In classrooms that foster a growth mindset, educators create an environment where failure is seen as a natural part of learning, not something to be feared or avoided. Teachers can help students reframe their failures by encouraging them to reflect on what went wrong, adjust their strategies, and try again. This process of trial, reflection, and improvement is crucial for developing both academic skills and emotional resilience. Through this approach, students learn that their potential is not defined by their past performances, but by their ability to keep pushing forward and learning from every experience.

The Role of Mindset in Education

Mindset theory provides a powerful framework for educators to rethink how they approach teaching, feedback, and curriculum design. Here are three key ways mindset impacts education:

1. **Awareness of Personal Mindsets:** Both educators and students benefit from understanding their own mindsets. When teachers recognize whether they tend toward a fixed or growth mindset, they can work to reframe their beliefs and model a growth-oriented approach. Similarly, students who become aware of their mindset can begin to challenge limiting beliefs and adopt a more positive view of their abilities.

The science behind a growth mindset is rooted in the field of neuroscience, which shows that the brain is far more adaptable than we once believed. When students engage in learning and practice, neural connections strengthen, a process known as **neuroplasticity**. This phenomenon supports the notion that intelligence is not fixed but can be developed over time. Research has shown that when students approach challenges with a growth mindset, they activate areas of the brain associated with effort, problem-solving, and perseverance, rather than simply relying on innate talent. This understanding can empower students, as they learn that consistent effort and practice not only improve their academic abilities but also foster cognitive growth. Teachers who emphasize this concept help students see setbacks not as failures, but as integral steps in the learning process, reinforcing the idea that their abilities can continually expand.

1. **Feedback and Language:** Teacher feedback plays a crucial role in shaping students' mindsets. Feedback that focuses on the process—such as effort, strategies, and persistence—rather than innate ability encourages a growth mindset. For instance, praising a student's effort in solving a challenging problem ("You worked hard to figure that out!") is more beneficial than praising their intelligence ("You're so smart!"). The language used by teachers and educational leaders should align with a growth mindset, emphasizing progress, effort, and learning over fixed labels.
2. **Curriculum Design:** A curriculum that incorporates growth mindset principles can help students develop resilience and a love for learning. Such a curriculum emphasizes challenges as opportunities, encourages reflection after setbacks, and integrates compassionate teaching practices. Educators can align mindset interventions with academic content to ensure that students see the relevance of growth mindset principles in their everyday learning.
3. **Compassion and the Growth Mindset:** The connection between mindset and compassion is profound. As explored in earlier chapters, compassionate teaching involves understanding and supporting students as they navigate challenges. A growth mindset compliments this approach by empowering students to view those challenges as opportunities for growth. Compassionate educators avoid labeling students based on fixed traits and instead focus on their potential to improve and succeed.

Moreover, cultivating a growth mindset extends beyond students—it applies to educators and leaders as well. Teachers, like students, must be compassionate toward themselves, recognizing that their own growth is an ongoing process. Mistakes, setbacks, and uncertainties are part of the teaching journey, especially during challenging times like the Covid-19 pandemic. By embracing a growth mindset, educators can remain resilient and continue to inspire their students.

Leadership and the Growth Mindset

Educational leaders play a critical role in fostering a growth mindset culture within schools and institutions. Leaders can model growth-oriented behaviours by:

2. Encouraging staff to take risks and innovate without fear of failure.
3. Providing professional development opportunities that emphasize learning and growth.

Integrating a growth mindset into classroom culture goes beyond simply teaching the concept of effort and resilience; it's about creating an environment where students feel empowered to take risks and embrace the learning process. Educators can cultivate this culture by celebrating incremental progress, encouraging collaboration, and fostering a sense of community. In classrooms where growth mindset principles are actively promoted, students are more likely to support each other's development, share strategies for overcoming difficulties, and celebrate each other's progress. Teachers can create activities that emphasize **cooperative learning**, where students work together to solve problems and reflect on their collective efforts. This sense of community and shared responsibility not only deepens students' understanding of the content but also builds a classroom culture centred on mutual respect, encouragement, and the shared belief that everyone is capable of growth.

Creating a supportive environment where teachers and students feel valued and empowered to improve.

Leadership that prioritizes growth mindsets can transform not only classrooms but entire educational communities, fostering collaboration, resilience, and a shared commitment to progress.

Practical Applications of the Growth Mindset

To integrate a growth mindset into educational settings, educators can adopt the following strategies:

1. **Model Growth-Oriented Behaviours**: Share personal stories of learning from mistakes and overcoming challenges. Show students that growth is a lifelong process.
2. **Teach About the Brain**: Help students understand how the brain can grow and adapt through learning. This knowledge can demystify intelligence and encourage students to embrace effort.
3. **Celebrate Effort and Progress:** Acknowledge students' hard work and improvement, even if they have not yet mastered a concept. This reinforces the value of persistence.
4. **Encourage Reflection:** Create opportunities for students to reflect on their learning processes, identify strategies that worked, and set goals for further growth.
5. **Align Curriculum with Mindset Principles:** Design lessons that challenge students at an appropriate level, provide opportunities for collaboration, and emphasize the value of perseverance.

Mindset as a Foundation for Growth

As Mercer (2012) aptly states, "The capacity of every learner to grow" depends on being provided with the right opportunities, contexts, support, environments, and time. Understanding mindsets is a fundamental step toward facilitating such growth. While individuals may differ in their natural predispositions, the belief in the potential for growth is universal.

By adopting a growth mindset, educators can help students develop resilience, confidence, and a love for learning. This approach not only enhances academic achievement but also prepares students for lifelong success. Furthermore, when educational leaders champion growth mindset principles, they create environments where teachers and students alike can thrive.

The concept of mindset, as introduced by Carol Dweck, offers educators a powerful tool to transform teaching and learning. By fostering a growth mindset culture, educators can help students and themselves embrace challenges, learn from failures, and reach their full potential. When combined with compassionate teaching, differentiation, and expertise, the growth mindset becomes a cornerstone of modern education—enabling students and teachers to navigate an ever-changing world with resilience, curiosity, and hope.

Chapter 12: The Art of Listening in Education

Listening is one of the most fundamental yet often overlooked skills in education. It is an act of connection, a bridge between individuals that fosters understanding, empathy, and mutual respect. In a world where distractions abound and the pace of life often leaves little room for reflection, the ability to truly listen has become more critical than ever. This chapter explores the transformative power of listening in education, emphasizing its role in building compassionate relationships, enhancing communication, and creating an environment where all voices are heard.

Building on previous chapters' themes of compassion, differentiation, and mindset, this chapter highlights how active listening can foster meaningful connections between teachers, students, and leaders. By prioritizing listening as a central component of educational practice, we can cultivate a culture of empathy, trust, and collaboration.

The Importance of Listening

Listening is far more than a passive activity—it requires focus, effort, and intention. As the Samaritans' work demonstrates, listening can be a lifeline for those in need, providing essential emotional support and validation. In education, the act of listening has the potential to transform relationships, build trust, and create a sense of belonging.

All too often, however, we fail to listen effectively. Research has shown that many of us fall victim to poor listening habits, such as:

1. Being selective about what we want to hear.
2. Becoming easily distracted during conversations.
3. Interrupting the speaker to steer the dialogue in a preferred direction.
4. Predicting what the speaker will say next and filtering their words through our assumptions.
5. Formulating responses before the speaker has finished talking.
6. Ignoring non-verbal cues, such as body language or tone of voice.

7. Speaking too soon to fill silences, thereby depriving others of the space to think and share fully.

These habits not only hinder meaningful communication but also prevent us from understanding others' perspectives. Psychotherapist Philippa Perry argues that many of these tendencies stem from our early experiences. If our feelings were not taken seriously as children, we may struggle to truly hear and validate others in adulthood. However, Perry also emphasizes that we can develop better listening skills by becoming more intentional, compassionate, and open to being influenced by others.

1. **Active Listening in Education**

   Active listening is a cornerstone of compassionate teaching. It involves not only hearing what is said but also paying attention to non-verbal cues, emotions, and silences. In the context of education, active listening can take many forms:

2. **Teachers Listening to Students**

   When teachers actively listen to their students, they create a classroom environment where students feel valued and understood. Listening allows teachers to identify students' needs, strengths, and challenges, enabling them to provide more effective support. Moreover, when students feel heard, they are more likely to engage in learning and build trust with their teachers.

3. **Students Listening to Teachers**

   Encouraging students to listen actively to their teachers fosters mutual respect and enhances the learning process. When students truly listen, they are better able to absorb information, ask meaningful questions, and participate in discussions. Teachers can model good listening behaviors to help students develop these skills.

4. **Teachers Listening to Colleagues**

Collaboration among teachers is an essential element in fostering both professional growth and the development of more effective teaching practices. In today's rapidly evolving educational landscape, no teacher can afford to work in isolation. Through collaboration, teachers have the opportunity to exchange ideas, strategies, and insights, which can significantly enhance their own teaching methods. By actively engaging with colleagues, teachers gain fresh perspectives that may challenge their current approaches, helping them to identify areas for improvement or adopt innovative strategies that better meet the needs of their students.

Active listening is a key component of this collaborative process. When teachers listen attentively to their colleagues, they create a space for open dialogue and idea-sharing. This not only enriches their own teaching but also promotes a culture of mutual respect and continuous learning within the school. By carefully considering the viewpoints and experiences of others, teachers can gain valuable insights that may otherwise have gone unnoticed, broadening their understanding of how to approach different teaching challenges.

In addition to professional growth, collaboration also plays a critical role in fostering a strong sense of community among educators. When teachers come together to share their successes, struggles, and strategies, they build a supportive network where they can rely on each other for guidance, encouragement, and feedback. This sense of camaraderie strengthens the overall work environment, making it easier for educators to navigate the challenges they face in their classrooms.

Furthermore, collaboration provides a constructive approach to resolving conflicts. Disagreements or differing opinions are inevitable in any workplace, but through collaborative communication, teachers can work through these issues in a respectful and solution-oriented manner. Active listening ensures that all parties feel heard and valued, paving the way for more effective conflict resolution. By understanding the perspectives of others and seeking common ground, teachers can foster stronger working relationships, which, in turn, contribute to a more positive and productive school culture.

Ultimately, collaboration is a cornerstone of professional development. By actively participating in collaborative activities such as peer observations, team teaching, or professional learning communities, teachers are not only improving their own practice but also contributing to the broader educational community. This ongoing exchange of knowledge and support ensures that teaching practices remain dynamic and responsive to the needs of both students and educators.

Leaders Listening to Teachers and Students

Educational leaders play a vital role in shaping the culture of schools and institutions. By listening to teachers and students, leaders can make more informed decisions, address concerns, and create policies that reflect the needs of the community. Listening also demonstrates respect and empathy, qualities that are essential for effective leadership.

A Culture of Listening

Imagine an educational system where listening is prioritized at all levels—students listening to teachers, teachers listening to students, teachers listening to one another, and leaders listening to the entire school community. Such a culture would foster collaboration, understanding, and a shared commitment to growth and improvement.

The Practice of Compassionate Listening

To become better listeners, educators and leaders must embrace a compassionate model of listening. Compassionate listening involves:

1. **Being Present:** Fully focusing on the speaker without distractions.
2. **Empathy:** Understanding and validating the speaker's emotions and perspectives.
3. **Non-Judgment:** Listening without forming conclusions or criticisms.

4. **Silence:** Allowing pauses and silences to create space for deeper reflection.
5. **Openness:** Being willing to be influenced by what the speaker shares, even if it challenges our assumptions.

By adopting these practices, educators can create a safe and supportive environment where all voices are heard and valued.

The Impact of Listening

Listening is not just a skill—it is an act of care and connection. In the world of education, listening can have profound effects:

1. **For Students:** When students feel heard, they are more likely to engage in learning, take risks, and develop confidence.
2. **For Teachers:** Listening fosters collaboration, reduces misunderstandings, and enhances professional relationships.
3. **For Leaders:** Listening helps leaders make more informed decisions, build trust, and create a positive school culture.
4. **For the Educational Community:** A culture of listening promotes empathy, respect, and understanding, creating a more inclusive and compassionate educational environment.

Conclusion

The Transformative Power of Listening in Education

Listening is a simple yet profoundly powerful act that holds the potential to revolutionize the way we experience and engage with education. It is often an overlooked skill, but when practiced with intention and compassion, listening can lead to remarkable outcomes in the classroom and beyond. Educators and leaders who prioritize **active and compassionate listening** foster stronger relationships, promote mutual understanding, and create a welcoming environment where every individual feels valued and supported. As the Samaritans wisely remind us, "listening can save lives." In the context of education, listening holds the power to **transform lives**—both for students and educators alike.

Imagine a world where listening is not just a passive activity but an active, meaningful practice woven into the fabric of daily interactions. In such a world, **students listen to their teachers** not merely to absorb information, but to feel heard and understood. **Teachers listen to their students**, not just to assess their academic progress but to acknowledge their struggles, joys, and unique perspectives. **Colleagues listen to one another**, offering support and advice without judgment, creating an atmosphere of collaboration rather than competition. **Leaders listen to their communities**, ensuring that decisions reflect the needs and voices of those they serve. This world is not a distant dream; it is entirely possible—and it begins with the conscious choice to listen.

At its core, **listening is an act of connection**. It's more than simply hearing words; it's about understanding the intent behind those words, the emotions that accompany them, and the context in which they are spoken. In a classroom or educational setting, active listening creates a bridge between individuals, helping them connect on a deeper level. For students, feeling listened to increases their sense of self-worth, boosts confidence, and improves their ability to engage in learning. For teachers, listening to their students fosters empathy, strengthens their instructional approaches, and cultivates a more supportive teaching environment.

As educators, we must commit to becoming **better listeners**—not just as a professional skill, but as a core value of our practice. This means making a deliberate effort to **listen attentively**, without distractions, to truly understand what others are saying. It involves giving others the space to express their thoughts and feelings, especially when they may feel hesitant or vulnerable. Creating **safe spaces** where every voice matters and every story is heard should be a priority in every school, classroom, and educational environment. When we listen deeply, we show that we value others as individuals, not just as students or colleagues.

In the act of listening, we discover the immense power of **compassion**. Listening with empathy and without judgment creates opportunities for growth and healing, whether in a challenging lesson, a difficult conversation, or a moment of emotional support. It allows for the exchange of ideas, nurtures understanding, and fosters a sense of belonging. Through active listening, educators create an environment where both **students and teachers grow together**, where learning is not just about the exchange of facts, but about shared experiences and mutual respect. It is in this environment that true transformation happens—because listening does more than just communicate understanding; it deepens the connections that form the foundation of effective education.

Ultimately, when we listen with purpose and compassion, we build not only stronger individuals but stronger communities. We give our students and colleagues the space to thrive, to feel valued, and to express their thoughts, dreams, and concerns. In doing so, we create an educational ecosystem where growth is not a solitary experience but a collective journey. The choice to listen is not just an act of kindness—it's an act of empowerment. It's a commitment to **building a better world**—one conversation at a time.

Chapter 13: Braving the Wilderness in Education

Education is often described as a journey—a path of discovery, growth, and connection. But sometimes, this journey requires us to step off the well-trodden path and venture into the wilderness, a space where we confront discomfort, uncertainty, and vulnerability. Brené Brown's concept of "braving the wilderness" resonates deeply with the challenges educators face in staying true to themselves and fostering authentic relationships in a data-driven, pressure-filled world. Brown (2017) writes, "When we are willing to risk venturing into the wilderness, and even becoming our own wilderness, we feel the deepest connection to our true self and to what matters the most."

This chapter explores the idea of braving the wilderness within the context of education. It builds on previous chapters discussing compassion, mindset, and listening, emphasizing the importance of authenticity, vulnerability, and relationship-driven practices in teaching, learning, and leadership. By prioritizing connection over conformity, educators can cultivate environments where both they and their students can thrive.

The Wilderness of Authenticity

For many educators, the staffroom can feel like a microcosm of the broader educational system—a place where conversations about policies, challenges, and frustrations unfold. While these discussions can be cathartic, they sometimes create an atmosphere of negativity that stifles optimism and innovation. For those who hold a more positive or hopeful perspective, expressing their views can feel like stepping into the wilderness—a place of potential isolation and risk.

True belonging, as Brené Brown describes, requires authenticity. It demands that we stand firm in our beliefs and values, even when they differ from those around us. This is no easy feat in education, where the desire for connection and acceptance among colleagues can sometimes lead to self-silencing. The fear of being judged, misunderstood, or excluded can prevent educators from speaking their truth.

During the pandemic, one educator had a profound realization that forever changed their approach to their professional relationships.

They reflected, "If I want to relate authentically with my colleagues, I am going to have to stand up and tell them the truth about my position in things." This simple yet powerful statement marks the moment when they decided to embrace authenticity over the comfort of conformity. The pandemic, with its whirlwind of uncertainty and rapid change, became the backdrop for this shift in perspective.

In stepping into the "wilderness" of vulnerability, this educator faced the fear of judgment, potential rejection, and the discomfort of being truly seen. But it was within this very wilderness that they discovered a space for deeper, more genuine connections with their colleagues. Rather than hiding behind the veil of politeness or keeping their thoughts to themselves out of fear of conflict, they chose to speak their truth—honestly, openly, and with respect.

The bravery required to do this was not just about speaking up; it was about embracing the risk of being misunderstood or excluded in order to honor their own voice. In doing so, this educator found a way to foster an environment where authenticity could flourish, where colleagues could share their truths without the burden of pretending to fit in. By choosing authenticity, they not only honored their own experiences and beliefs but also created a space where others felt encouraged to do the same. This openness paved the way for more meaningful interactions and stronger professional bonds, as each person, liberated from the fear of judgment, was able to engage more fully, more sincerely, and more humanly.

Relationship-Driven Education

Perhaps the world of education should not be data-driven, but relationship-driven. At its core, education is about human connection—the bonds between teachers and students, colleagues, and communities. Brené Brown's work emphasizes the innate human desire for connection and belonging, a desire that is no less critical in the professional world of education than it is in the personal sphere.

When educators prioritize relationships, they create environments where trust, respect, and collaboration can flourish. This requires vulnerability, the willingness to be seen and heard as you truly are. It also requires active listening, as discussed in the previous chapter, and the courage to engage in honest, open dialogue.

In a relationship-driven model of education, the following principles are key:

1. **Authenticity**: Teachers, leaders, and students are encouraged to express their true selves without fear of judgment or rejection.
2. **Empathy**: Understanding and valuing others' perspectives fosters trust and connection.
3. **Mutual Respect**: Relationships are built on a foundation of respect for diverse opinions and experiences.
4. **Collaboration**: Everyone in the educational community—students, teachers, and leaders—works together to create a shared vision for learning and growth.

The Role of Vulnerability in Leadership

Educational leaders, in particular, face the challenge of braving the wilderness. As decision-makers and role models, leaders often feel pressure to present a confident, unshakable front. Yet vulnerability is a strength, not a weakness, in leadership. When leaders are willing to admit uncertainty, share their struggles, and invite others into the conversation, they create a culture of trust and openness.

For example, a school principal who acknowledges the challenges of adapting to new policies or navigating a crisis like the Covid-19 pandemic demonstrates humility and humanity. By sharing their own experiences and listening to the concerns of staff and students, the leader fosters a sense of solidarity and shared purpose.

Building Resilient Professional Relationships

One of the most profound and rewarding outcomes of venturing into the wilderness of authenticity is the chance to cultivate resilient and dynamic relationships with colleagues. These relationships, rooted in mutual understanding and a shared willingness to support one another through both the mundane and the challenging moments, are the bedrock of a thriving educational community.

In these relationships, openness is key—a genuine openness to listen, to truly hear what others are saying, and to respect diverse perspectives. It's about embracing the idea that every individual has a unique viewpoint shaped by their experiences, and that this diversity should be welcomed, not stifled. When we allow our relationships to evolve, when we give space for growth and change, we create a fertile ground for collaboration and innovation.

Even when our opinions diverge, when the debates are heated or when disagreements arise, it's in those moments that the true strength of these relationships becomes evident. By engaging in honest and respectful dialogue, rather than avoiding the tough conversations, we strengthen our connections with one another. These conversations, though at times uncomfortable, open the door to deeper understanding and empathy, forging a bond that is more robust and more meaningful.

In a professional setting, this sense of connection goes far beyond simply working together—it fosters a genuine sense of belonging. When we feel that our voices are heard and our opinions valued, we are more likely to engage fully and invest in the collective success of the team. The willingness to stand by one another, to offer support during difficult times, and to celebrate each other's victories strengthens the foundation of trust upon which these resilient relationships are built.

Ultimately, these relationships are not just about professional collaboration; they are about creating a space where people feel safe, valued, and understood. In this space, we thrive not only as colleagues but as individuals, knowing that we are part of something greater than ourselves—a community that supports each other, grows together, and faces challenges with unwavering solidarity.

Lessons for Educators

Braving the wilderness in education requires courage, empathy, and a commitment to authenticity. Here are some practical ways educators can navigate this journey:

1. **Speak Your Truth with Respect**: Share your perspectives openly, but do so in a way that honors the views of others.

2. **Listen Actively**: As discussed in Chapter 12, listening is a powerful tool for building understanding and connection.
3. **Embrace Discomfort**: Stepping into the wilderness means confronting discomfort and uncertainty. See these moments as opportunities for growth.
4. **Foster a Culture of Belonging**: Create spaces where all voices are valued, and where everyone feels seen and heard.
5. **Lead with Vulnerability**: Whether in the classroom or in leadership roles, model openness and authenticity for others.

The Wilderness as a Space for Growth

The wilderness, as Brené Brown describes it, is not a place of isolation but of transformation. It is where we confront our fears, challenge our assumptions, and connect with our true selves. In the world of education, venturing into the wilderness allows us to build deeper relationships, foster a sense of belonging, and create environments where everyone—students, teachers, and leaders—can thrive.

By prioritizing authenticity, compassion, and connection, we can reimagine education as a relationship-driven journey, one where braving the wilderness is not just an act of courage but a path to growth and fulfillment.

Chapter 14: The Role of Discipline in Education

Discipline is often misunderstood as an imposition of external rules or restrictions, a concept that many views with resistance or even fear. However, as Jim Collins outlines in his book *Good to Great* (2001), true discipline is not about external orders but about internal responsibility. It involves disciplined people engaging in disciplined thought and taking disciplined action within a framework of freedom and accountability. This culture of discipline, when infused with creativity and purpose, creates the foundation for greatness.

In the context of education, discipline is not only about classroom management or enforcing rules but also about cultivating the self-discipline necessary for students, teachers, and leaders to achieve their goals. Discipline, when approached with compassion and understanding, becomes a cornerstone of learning, growth, and resilience. Building on themes from previous chapters—such as mindset, listening, and authenticity—this chapter explores how discipline can be nurtured in educational settings to foster persistence, focus, and long-term success.

At its core, discipline is the ability to govern one's own actions, even in the face of resistance. It involves acting with intention and focus, rather than being swayed by distractions or external obstacles. Self-discipline allows individuals to overcome internal and external challenges, enabling them to persist in their efforts toward meaningful goals.

David C. Geary, an evolutionary psychologist, highlights the importance of discipline in learning. He distinguishes between primary learning—skills that are intuitive and easily acquired through play and exploration—and secondary learning, which requires effort, focus, and the engagement of working memory. Secondary learning, such as mastering reading, writing, or algebra, is not something the brain is naturally structured to do with ease. It demands discipline to push through the resistance and discomfort that come with deep thinking and complex problem-solving.

Without discipline, learners may gravitate toward the path of least resistance, relying on intuitive but superficial understanding. While primary learning is important, it is insufficient for achieving higher-order thinking skills and academic success. True learning requires the deliberate effort to engage with challenging material, reflect deeply, and persist in the face of frustration.

The Discipline of Teaching and Learning

Discipline is not just for students—it is equally essential for teachers and leaders. In the classroom, discipline manifests in the structures and practices that teachers implement to create an environment conducive to learning. This includes:

1. **Providing Clear Structures**: Just as learners need discipline to engage with challenging material, teachers must provide the scaffolding that supports this process. Clear expectations, well-organized lessons, and consistent routines help students focus their attention and develop self-discipline over time.
2. **Modeling Discipline**: Teachers who demonstrate self-discipline in their own actions—whether through preparation, punctuality, or perseverance—set a powerful example for their students. By modeling disciplined thought and behavior, educators inspire their students to adopt similar habits.
3. **Balancing Challenge and Support**: Effective teaching requires the discipline to push students out of their comfort zones while providing the support they need to succeed. This balance fosters resilience, persistence, and a growth mindset.

Compassionate Discipline

Discipline does not have to be harsh or punitive. When approached with compassion, discipline becomes a tool for empowering students to take responsibility for their learning. Compassionate discipline involves understanding students' struggles, encouraging their efforts, and celebrating their progress.

Before we dive into specific strategies for developing self-discipline in students, it's important to recognize that self-discipline is not something that comes naturally to everyone. It is, in fact, a skill that can be nurtured and strengthened over time. Just as we practice math, reading, or any other academic subject, self-discipline requires continuous effort and intentional practice. It's a journey of building habits, adjusting mindsets, and gradually developing the tools to stay focused, resilient, and goal-oriented, even in the face of distractions or adversity.

As educators, our role is not only to teach content but also to foster the mental and emotional habits that contribute to self-discipline. This means creating an environment where students feel supported, challenged, and encouraged to take responsibility for their learning. We must help them understand that self-discipline is about more than just following rules—it's about developing the inner strength to make choices that align with their long-term goals, even when short-term temptations or difficulties arise. In this way, self-discipline becomes not just a skill for school, but a lifelong tool that students can carry with them into all areas of life.

Developing Self-Discipline in Students

The good news is that self-discipline is not an innate trait—it can be cultivated. Educators play a crucial role in helping students develop the habits and mindsets necessary for disciplined action. Here are some strategies for fostering self-discipline in students:

1. **Teach the Value of Effort**: Emphasize the importance of persistence and effort in achieving goals. Help students understand that success is not about avoiding discomfort but about working through resistance to reach new levels of understanding.
2. **Encourage Goal Setting**: Guide students in setting realistic, achievable goals and breaking them into smaller, manageable steps. This helps them stay focused and motivated over the long term.
3. **Create Opportunities for Reflection**: Encourage students to reflect on their progress and challenges. Reflection helps them develop self-awareness and learn from their experiences.
4. **Promote Mindful Focus**: Teach students strategies for staying present and focused, such as mindfulness exercises or techniques for managing distractions.

5. **Celebrate Progress**: Acknowledge and celebrate students' efforts and achievements, reinforcing the value of disciplined action.

The Intersection of Discipline and Compassion

While discipline requires effort and perseverance, it should never be equated with rigidity or harshness. In fact, discipline and compassion go hand in hand. A disciplined approach to teaching and learning is most effective when it is grounded in empathy, curiosity, and generosity.

Compassionate discipline recognizes the human side of education. It acknowledges that students, teachers, and leaders all face challenges and that growth is a continuous journey. By combining self-discipline with self-compassion, individuals can navigate setbacks with resilience, maintain their sense of authenticity, and stay focused on their goals.

This integrated approach to discipline aligns with the broader themes explored in this book, including the importance of fostering a growth mindset, listening with empathy, and building authentic relationships. Discipline, when practiced with compassion, becomes a tool for empowerment rather than a source of stress or control.

This approach to discipline shifts the focus from compliance to personal responsibility, allowing students, teachers, and leaders to take ownership of their learning and growth. When discipline is coupled with a growth mindset, individuals begin to see challenges not as obstacles but as opportunities to learn and improve. They are more likely to persist through difficulties, viewing mistakes as part of the journey rather than setbacks. This mindset transforms discipline from a rigid requirement to a pathway toward self-improvement, helping individuals build the resilience needed to tackle future challenges.

Furthermore, when discipline is practiced with empathy, it nurtures a deeper sense of understanding within the educational community. Empathy allows educators to see students as whole individuals with unique struggles and strengths, guiding them with patience and kindness. Instead of responding to behaviors with frustration or punishment, empathetic discipline seeks to understand the root causes of a student's actions, providing support that addresses their needs while maintaining high expectations for growth. This compassionate approach fosters trust and creates a safe space for students to develop their self-discipline without fear of judgment or failure.

Ultimately, discipline, when rooted in empathy and a growth mindset, leads to stronger, more authentic relationships. As educators, model disciplined thought and behavior, they not only help students become more focused and goal-oriented but also build meaningful connections that go beyond the classroom. These relationships are grounded in mutual respect and understanding, allowing both students and teachers to flourish in an environment where personal growth is celebrated and the pursuit of excellence is shared. When discipline is framed as a tool for empowerment, it transforms the entire learning experience into one that is collaborative, supportive, and oriented toward long-term success.

The Rewards of Discipline

Discipline pays off in countless ways. For students, it opens the door to deeper learning, higher achievement, and greater confidence. For teachers and leaders, it enhances their ability to create meaningful, lasting impact in their educational communities. For all individuals, discipline fosters qualities such as persistence, resilience, and adaptability, enabling them to overcome obstacles and achieve their goals.

As Jim Collins suggests, disciplined people who engage in disciplined thought and action create a culture of greatness. In education, this culture of discipline can transform classrooms, schools, and institutions, inspiring everyone involved to reach their full potential.

Discipline is not about restriction or control—it is about freedom within responsibility. It is the foundation for achieving excellence in education and in life. By fostering self-discipline in ourselves and our students, we create the conditions for growth, resilience, and success. As educators, let us embrace the power of disciplined thought and action, not as a burden but as a gift. Let us approach discipline with compassion, curiosity, and generosity, knowing that it holds the key to unlocking the potential within every learner, teacher, and leader. With discipline as our guide, we can navigate even the most challenging terrain and achieve greatness together.

Chapter 15: Love, Recovery, and the Measure of Education's Worth

Education is not merely an institution; it is a living, breathing force that shapes individuals, communities, and nations. Its impact can be measured in tangible terms, such as increased productivity and higher wages, but its true value lies in the intangible: the confidence it builds, the passions it ignites, and the lives it transforms. Education is one deeply personal and profoundly societal. It represents love for knowledge, recovery from setbacks, and the resilience needed to adapt to an ever-changing world.

This chapter explores the multifaceted value of education by weaving together measurable outcomes, personal narratives, and the emotional culture that sustains learning. Building on previous chapters' themes of compassion, listening, discipline, and authenticity, it highlights how education is both a metric of progress and a personal journey of growth, love, and recovery.

Education's true power lies not only in the academic knowledge it imparts but, in its ability, to inspire individuals to reach their fullest potential. It is a dynamic, evolving force that adapts to the needs of both learners and society. While standardized testing and graduation rates offer a snapshot of progress, they only scratch the surface of what education truly offers. Education cultivates curiosity, shapes values, and fosters the drive for continual growth. It is through the process of learning that individuals gain the tools to face the world with confidence, empathy, and a commitment to lifelong discovery.

Moreover, the impact of education extends beyond the individual. It ripples out to affect families, communities, and even entire nations. A well-educated populace contributes not only to economic advancement but also to social cohesion and cultural enrichment. The connections forged within educational environments—whether between student and teacher, peers, or communities—create networks of support that help individuals recover from failures, navigate challenges, and build resilience. Education, when approached holistically, transforms both individuals and society, enabling people to adapt, thrive, and contribute meaningfully to the ever-changing world around them.

The Measurable Value of Education

While the tangible benefits of education, such as higher wages and increased productivity, are often the primary focus of policymakers and governments, it's essential to remember that the true worth of education cannot be fully captured by numbers alone. Education plays a central role in shaping individuals' lives, empowering them with the knowledge, skills, and confidence to navigate an increasingly complex world. It is a powerful tool that not only prepares people for careers but also equips them with the critical thinking, creativity, and emotional intelligence needed to succeed in life. The broader societal impact of education reaches far beyond the workforce—it is foundational to fostering informed, engaged citizens who contribute to the social, cultural, and economic well-being of their communities.

Governments and policymakers often evaluate education through the lens of quantifiable outcomes. According to the Department for Education (Measuring the Worth of Education, 2021), the value of education can be seen in the increase in productivity in learner performance as a result of achieving relevant qualifications. Higher qualifications often lead to higher wages, effectively doubling the productivity gains by benefiting both the learner and society.

This measurable impact is significant. Education equips individuals with the skills and knowledge needed to contribute to the workforce, innovate within industries, and drive economic growth. It underscores education's role as a cornerstone of societal advancement. Yet, while these outcomes are important, they cannot fully encapsulate education's transformative power. Beyond wages and productivity, education is deeply personal—it changes lives in ways that statistics cannot measure.

What Education Did for Me: A Personal Journey

To truly understand the value of education, one must get personal. Education is not just about qualifications or economic outcomes; it is about the moments, mentors, and lessons that shape who we are.

1. **Inspiration and Confidence:** At secondary school, a Latin teacher instilled confidence in me, encouraging me to believe I could attend university and pursue a degree in Teaching Spanish. This belief became a foundation for my educational journey.
2. **A Love for Literature:** At the University of Granada, Luis García Montero introduced me to the beauty of literature and the works of Federico García Lorca, sparking a lifelong passion for writing and critical thought.
3. **Belonging and Purpose:** During my teacher training year, I learned what it meant to be part of something larger than myself—a shared mission to educate and inspire.
4. **Ethics and Independence:** Later, while completing my Master's in Education at Nottingham Trent University, Sue Wallace taught me the importance of ethical research and independent thinking, deepening my love for learning and teaching.

Through education, I found my passion, my path, and a sense of direction for life. It gave me the tools to connect with people of diverse backgrounds, embrace new ideas, and contribute meaningfully to the world.

The Role of Love in Education

Education is not only about intellectual growth; it is also a space where emotional connections are formed. Research by Barsade and O'Neill (*What's Love Got to Do With It?*, 2014) highlights the importance of an emotional culture of compassionate love in workplaces. This type of love—characterized by care, compassion, and kindness—leads to greater satisfaction, teamwork, and positive outcomes.

In educational settings, companionate love is equally transformative. It fosters:

1. **Caring for Others:** Recognizing the humanity in every individual, whether it's a struggling student, a burnt-out teacher, or a colleague in need of support.

2. **Empathy in Action:** Listening, understanding, and responding to the needs of others with compassion and attentiveness.
3. **Commitment to Growth:** Believing in the potential of every learner and colleague to grow, improve, and succeed.

When love is at the heart of education, it creates an environment where individuals feel safe, valued, and supported. It strengthens relationships, builds trust, and helps communities navigate challenges together.

The Necessity of Recovery

Education, like any human endeavor, is not immune to setbacks. The Covid-19 pandemic exposed the vulnerabilities of educational systems worldwide, leading to disruptions in learning, increased mental health challenges, and systemic inequities. As *The Spectator* (2021) reported, the long-term consequences of these disruptions could remain with learners for life if not addressed.

Recovery in education requires more than superficial fixes, such as adjusted exam standards or temporary policies. It demands a commitment to addressing root causes, rebuilding trust, and prioritizing the well-being of students and educators alike.

Repairing what is Broken

In education, mistakes, failures, and setbacks are an unavoidable part of the process. Whether it's a missed opportunity for a lesson, an unplanned disruption in the classroom, or systemic challenges that hinder progress, the reality is that imperfections are inherent in any learning environment. However, what truly defines the success of an educational system is not the absence of mistakes, but how we respond to them. Every error provides an opportunity for growth, reflection, and improvement, which, when approached with the right mindset, can be transformative for both educators and students.

As one educator wisely reflected, "It is not the mistakes that matter so much, because we all do them; it is how to put them right." This mindset highlights the importance of resilience and problem-solving. It's about recognizing where things have gone wrong, accepting responsibility, and taking meaningful action to correct course. In educational contexts, this process of repairing can take many forms: whether it's revisiting and revising teaching strategies, providing additional support to struggling students, or creating a culture where failure is seen as an essential part of learning rather than a permanent setback. When mistakes are met with a commitment to repair and improve, they become stepping stones to greater understanding, better outcomes, and a more compassionate, resilient educational environment. This willingness to confront mistakes head-on fosters a culture of growth, where individuals are not afraid to make mistakes, but empowered to learn from them and emerge stronger.

Recovery begins with:

1. **Awareness:** Recognizing the warning signs of decline, whether in student performance, teacher well-being, or institutional integrity.
2. **Accountability:** Taking responsibility for mistakes and poor decisions instead of ignoring problems or shifting blame.
3. **Action:** Implementing thoughtful, compassionate strategies to repair damage and rebuild progress.

Recovery also requires a cultural shift. For too long, educational environments have perpetuated a hierarchical, perfectionist mindset where admitting mistakes is seen as a weakness. To foster recovery, we must create spaces where vulnerability is safe, forgiveness is practiced, and learning from failure is celebrated.

Balancing Love, Recovery, and Measurable Outcomes

Education's value lies at the intersection of measurable outcomes, emotional connection, and personal growth. While qualifications and productivity metrics are important, they are only part of the story. Education is also about the love that inspires learning, the recovery that follows setbacks, and the personal journeys that transform lives.

A balanced approach to education requires:

1. **Companionate Love:** Placing care, empathy, and relational connection at the center of teaching and learning.
2. **Resilience and Recovery:** Acknowledging failures, addressing challenges, and striving for continuous improvement.
3. **Measuring What Matters:** Valuing not only economic outcomes but also the intangible benefits of education, such as confidence, creativity, and connection.

The Legacy of Education

No educational system, teacher, or learner is immune to failure, but the true measure of education lies in its capacity to recover, adapt, and grow stronger. Education is not just a means to an end; it is a journey filled with love, resilience, and transformation.

As we continue to build and rebuild our educational systems, let us remember that education is more than qualifications and wages. It is the teacher who inspires confidence, the mentor who fosters passion, and the community that supports recovery. It is, above all, an act of love—a belief that every learner has the potential to grow, and every system has the capacity to transform.

As we look to the future of education, it is essential to recognize that the legacy of education is not defined solely by academic achievements or economic success. It is defined by the relationships it builds, the opportunities it creates for growth, and the lasting impact it has on individuals and communities. Every lesson taught, every challenge overcome, and every moment of support and encouragement contributes to the broader narrative of human development. Education empowers individuals to realize their full potential, but it also fosters a collective sense of purpose, where communities grow stronger through shared learning and mutual support.

The true legacy of education is the ripple effect it creates—one where the values of resilience, empathy, and empowerment are passed down to future generations. As educators, leaders, and learners, we have the opportunity to shape this legacy, ensuring that the educational journey is one of continuous transformation. Education teaches us that growth is not linear, and setbacks do not define us; instead, it is how we respond to adversity and continue to push forward that ultimately shapes our future. By fostering environments that nurture both intellectual and emotional development, we lay the foundation for a future where education remains a powerful tool for personal and societal transformation, bringing us closer to a more compassionate and resilient world.

Chapter 16: Lifelong Learning and the Integration of Jungian Principles in Teacher Development

Education is often regarded as a finite process—an endeavor that culminates in formal qualifications, a career, or a particular life stage. However, as Carl Jung asserts, this perspective is profoundly limited. Lifelong learning is not merely a choice; it is a necessity for navigating the complexities of adulthood and achieving personal and professional fulfillment (Jung, 1981). For educators, in particular, the journey of learning must continue beyond initial teacher training or qualifications. Teachers who embrace lifelong learning become better equipped to foster meaningful, empathetic, and creative learning environments for their students.

This chapter explores the potential of integrating Jungian principles into Continual Professional Development (CPD) for teachers in the UK. Drawing from Jung's insights on adult education, the chapter examines the practical and ethical challenges of this integration while highlighting the transformative potential it holds for teachers, students, and educational systems. Building on the themes of recovery, discipline, love, and the personal value of education from previous chapters, this discussion underscores the importance of reflective practice, self-awareness, and ongoing growth in the field of education.

Jung's Vision: Education Beyond Formal Schooling

Jung's perspective on education challenges the traditional, linear model of learning that views education as a finite process, concluding once formal schooling is complete. He highlights that education should not be seen as an endpoint, but rather as a continuous, evolving journey. According to Jung, true education extends beyond acquiring job-specific skills or achieving social milestones like marriage—it is a lifelong process that encompasses personal growth, self-awareness, and the development of a deeper understanding of the world. This view invites a broader conception of learning, one that transcends academic qualifications and addresses the ongoing need for intellectual and emotional growth throughout adulthood.

In *Child Development and Education* (Jung, 1981), Jung critiques the traditional view of education as something that ends with formal schooling. He writes, "We educate people only up to the point where they can earn a living and marry; the education ceases altogether, as though a complete mental outfit had been acquired." (Jung, 1981, par. 10). Jung argues that this superficial endpoint leaves individuals ill-equipped for the challenges of adult life, resulting in widespread personal and professional dissatisfaction.

For educators, this critique highlights the need for lifelong learning. Teachers who stop growing themselves risk stagnation, which can lead to repetitive, uninspired teaching and diminished engagement in the classroom. Conversely, teachers who pursue self-knowledge and personal development become more creative, reflective, and effective. They bring a richness to their teaching that inspires students to think critically, explore their potential, and connect deeply with the world around them.

The Potential of Jungian Principles in CPD

Jungian principles, particularly those related to self-awareness, creativity, and individuation, could significantly enhance CPD for teachers. By fostering a deeper understanding of themselves and their students, teachers could create more meaningful, empathetic, and engaging learning environments.

Potential Benefits:

1. **More Creative and Engaging Teaching:** Jung's emphasis on introspection and unconscious knowledge could encourage teachers to think beyond standardized methods and develop innovative approaches to teaching.
2. **Enhanced Student-Teacher Relationships:** Understanding Jung's theories on psychic disturbances and emotional well-being could help teachers better support their students' mental and emotional health.
3. **Reflective Practice:** Teachers who engage with Jungian principles may become more reflective practitioners, capable of analyzing their own biases, behaviors, and teaching styles to foster growth and improvement.

However, implementing these principles in CPD is not without challenges.

Practical Challenges

Integrating Jungian principles into CPD sessions presents significant practical hurdles:

1. **Complexity of Jung's Theories:** Jung's concepts, such as individuation, dream analysis, and the unconscious, are deeply psychological and require specialized understanding. Teachers would need extensive training to apply these principles effectively, which could strain resources and time.
2. **Need for Skilled Facilitators:** Schools and educational institutions would need expert professionals trained in Jungian analytical psychology. This specialized expertise would come at a significant cost, which many institutions may not be able to afford.
3. **Rigid Educational Systems:** Traditional education in the UK often prioritizes rational, standardized approaches, leaving little room for introspective or indirect methods of learning. Jung's ideas may clash with these entrenched systems.

The rigidity of traditional educational systems often leaves little room for the type of introspective, holistic learning that Jungian principles advocate. Standardized testing, rigid curricula, and the emphasis on measurable outcomes frequently overshadow the importance of emotional, psychological, and spiritual development. Jung's ideas, which encourage teachers to delve into self-awareness, unconscious material, and the deeper dimensions of human experience, challenge these conventional structures. This is not to say that rational and standardized methods are inherently flawed, but rather that they should be complemented by an approach that nurtures the inner growth of educators, fostering a richer, and more meaningful connection to both the profession and their students.

To integrate Jungian principles effectively within such a system, educators and administrators must challenge the status quo and adopt more flexible, inclusive frameworks. These frameworks would recognize that true learning encompasses not just cognitive knowledge but emotional and psychological growth as well. Teachers would benefit from opportunities to explore their own inner landscapes, enabling them to better understand the complexities of their students' experiences. By creating a more balanced, dynamic educational model that respects both the rational and the irrational, we can foster a system that nurtures the whole person—one that moves beyond merely teaching to the test and embraces the transformative power of self-discovery, creativity, and personal growth.

Jung himself acknowledged the challenges of interpreting unconscious material, noting that while some insights come intuitively, others require "much labour and considerable experience" (Jung, 1981, par. 114).

Ethical Considerations

Incorporating Jungian principles into CPD also raises ethical concerns:

1. **Privacy and Confidentiality:** Delving into unconscious material could expose sensitive personal information about teachers or students, raising questions about privacy.
2. **Boundaries of Professional Development:** Teachers may feel uncomfortable or unqualified to engage with psychological material, blurring the lines between education and therapy.
3. **Potential for Misuse:** Without proper training, there is a risk that Jungian principles could be misinterpreted or misapplied, leading to unintended harm.

To address these concerns, CPD programs would need to establish clear ethical guidelines, provide proper training, and ensure a supportive environment for teachers engaging with Jungian material.

Despite these challenges, integrating Jungian principles into CPD holds transformative potential. Jung's assertion that "the adult is educable" (Jung, 1981, par. 109) underscores the importance of embracing lifelong learning, not just for students but for educators as well.

The current educational paradigm is deeply inconsistent, as it fails to nurture the essential qualities of self-reflection and spiritual growth in both teachers and students. Otis's observation (1995) that insufficient time is allocated for students to engage in reflective practices is a symptom of a broader issue within teacher education, which often prioritizes indoctrination and compliance over meaningful professional development (Scruton, 1985). The lack of inward sensitivity and imagination among teachers, as Jung described results in a passive and unconscious acceptance of materials while taught by state mechanisms.

For effective professional development, the educational environment must provide conducive conditions that allow teachers to become aware of and align with the spirit of the time. With this awareness, educators' risk being influenced by unconscious political, economic, and personal forces. The journey toward self-knowledge and self-actualization cannot be measured through simplistic, linear evaluations but requires a recognition of the complex, non-linear nature of personal and professional growth (Dilon & Maguire, 1997).

As Mills (2024) suggests, the future of education hangs in the balance between being dominated by profit-driven private industry and becoming a state-controlled, no-cost system that values independent academic contributions. The current chaotic state of education stems from a lack of consensus on educational goals and a focus on superficial appearances rather than profound realities, as critiqued by Plato.

Instead of producing education that merely entertains or serves utilitarian purposes, we should aim for an education that reminds us of our deeper, spiritual nature. This involves a transformation of our being, achieved through ritual acts and the assimilation of the knower to the known, aligning with archetypal nature. The voice of the teacher, when properly trained and inspired, can communicate divine truths and foster metrical self-integration, as seen in Indian traditions. However, the prevailing system reduces education to a mechanical process, devoid of spiritual significance, leading to a perpetuation of superficiality and intellectualism without true fulfilment (Coomaraswamy, 1997).

Main considers that in education it is crucial to have "a vital connection to the mystery, meaningfulness, and sacredness of reality" (Main, 2022, p. 7). Otherwise, disenchantment, intellectualization, rationalization, and bureaucratization can continue to flourish in our educational settings, especially in our universities (Main, 2022).

Teachers who are actively involved in their own personal growth and self-discovery, maintaining a connection to their imaginative, emotional, and instinctual nature that relates to their true self, form a deep, almost subconscious bond with their students. This bond, which is different from that with the parents, benefits the child by creating a unique connection. This relationship helps protect the child's developing mind from the collective cultural pressures and ensures that their growing sense of self remains intact (Mitchell, 2019).

Proposed Directions for CPD:

After thoroughly reading Jung, considering current educational literature, and reflecting on my own experiences, it seems that the direction of Continuous Professional Development (CPD) for teachers in the UK should encompass the following points. Firstly, it should align with current research to dispel educational myths and address the cognitive, spiritual, psychological, and emotional needs of teachers. Secondly, it should encourage the exploration of education through both rational and irrational reasoning, emphasizing meaning, commitment, motivation, truth, revelation, and dreams. Thirdly, Continuous Professional Development should eliminate prejudices about inner and spiritual lives, allowing teachers to express their thoughts and accept the invisible and unprovable elements of human existence. Additionally, it should promote sharing practices and learning from other cultures to understand diverse ways of finding meaning and handling life's challenges. Providing opportunities for reflection on thoughts and emotions, supporting well-being through mindfulness and self-evaluation, is also crucial. Validating imagination, inspiration, and contemplation by encouraging connections within the curriculum should be a priority. Finally, education for adults should instill a mindset of inquiry and critical evaluation, focusing on character and personally developed while cultivating self-standards as an educational goal. By integrating these elements, the personal development of adult teachers can be more holistic and impactful, ultimately enhancing the growth of the educational sector.

Moreover, the integration of reflective practices within CPD should not be limited to occasional workshops or seminars but should be woven into the daily fabric of teaching. Teachers should be encouraged to engage in regular self-reflection, using tools such as journals or peer discussions to explore their teaching experiences, emotional responses, and professional growth. This continuous introspection will enable educators to better understand their own biases, assumptions, and emotional triggers, fostering a more compassionate, empathetic approach to teaching. Additionally, creating spaces for teachers to share their challenges and triumphs with peers can cultivate a collaborative and supportive environment that nurtures professional development on a deeper level. Such a culture of reflection can help teachers not only grow as educators but also evolve as individuals, finding greater meaning and satisfaction in their work.

Incorporating creativity and imagination into CPD programs can also play a crucial role in expanding the teaching toolkit. As Jung suggests, creativity is a key aspect of self-realization and individuation, and by allowing teachers to explore their creative potential, we can unlock new ways of thinking about teaching and learning. CPD that fosters creative expression—whether through art, storytelling, or innovative teaching methods—helps teachers reconnect with the joy and passion that led them to the profession in the first place. This not only enhances their own sense of fulfilment but also empowers them to bring that creativity into the classroom, where students can benefit from dynamic, engaging learning experiences that go beyond the confines of standard curricula.

Lastly, CPD should support teachers in cultivating a deep sense of purpose and commitment to their profession, beyond just the delivery of content. When educators are encouraged to explore the existential aspects of teaching—such as their role in shaping the next generation, their impact on society, and the broader ethical dimensions of education—they are more likely to remain motivated and inspired throughout their careers. By nurturing a sense of meaning in their work, CPD can help prevent burnout and create a sustainable career path for teachers. As they grow in their professional journey, teachers can become not only better educators but also more fulfilled, resilient individuals who contribute positively to their communities and the educational system as a whole.

Epilogue: The Lifelong Journey of Education

Education is an evolving tapestry, woven from the threads of theory, practice, personal growth, and societal transformation. Throughout this book, we have explored the intricate layers of education, from the strategies that promote inclusion in Modern Foreign Languages (MFL) classrooms to the broader philosophical and psychological principles that underpin effective teaching and learning. Each chapter has sought to illuminate the ways in which education is not only a tool for academic achievement but also a means of fostering connection, empathy, and resilience in both students and educators.

The first section of this book focused on the critical role of secondary education, particularly in the field of Modern Foreign Languages. We delved into strategies for creating inclusive classrooms, the importance of mentoring and leadership, and the innovative practices that can transform language learning into a meaningful and engaging experience. These chapters demonstrated that teaching languages is not just about grammar and vocabulary—it's about opening doors to new cultures, perspectives, and ways of thinking. By addressing the diverse needs of students and fostering positive teacher-student relationships, MFL educators can create environments where all learners feel valued and empowered to succeed.

The second section expanded the scope to explore broader themes in education and pedagogy. From navigating the challenges of differentiation and expertise to reflecting on the profound lessons of the Covid-19 pandemic, these chapters emphasized the adaptability and resilience required in modern education. Themes such as the power of mindset, the art of listening, and the role of love and discipline reminded us that education is as much about personal growth and emotional connection as it is about academic achievement. Finally, the integration of Carl Jung's principles into lifelong learning highlighted the transformative potential of education as a continuous journey of self-discovery and professional development.

As we conclude this exploration, it's clear that education isn't a finite process bound by the walls of the classroom or the years of formal schooling. It is a lifelong endeavour—one that evolves with the needs of society and the individual. Teachers are not just conveyors of knowledge; they are mentors, leaders, and catalysts for change. Likewise, students are not passive recipients of information but active participants in their own learning journeys.

The future of education lies in the ability to balance tradition with innovation, measurable outcomes with intangible growth, and structure with flexibility. It requires educators to embrace their own lifelong learning, to reflect on their practices, and to remain open to the ever-changing landscape of teaching and learning.

Ultimately, education is about more than curricula or qualifications—it is about empowering individuals to reach their full potential, fostering connections across cultures and communities, and preparing students to thrive in an increasingly complex world. It's about hope, growth, and transformation.

May this book serve as a guide, a reflection, and an inspiration for all who are committed to the transformative power of education. Whether you are a teacher, a leader, or a lifelong learner, remember that your journey in education is not just about the destination but about the meaningful steps you take along the way.

As we move forward, it is crucial to recognize that the future of education must be built on a foundation of continuous reflection and adaptability. In the ever-evolving landscape of technology, culture, and global interconnectedness, educators must cultivate the ability to adapt and grow along with their students. This involves not only learning new methodologies and embracing new technologies but also nurturing the emotional intelligence and resilience required to guide students through an uncertain world. The development of a global mindset, combined with the ability to empathize across cultural boundaries, will be essential in creating educational environments that are inclusive, dynamic, and responsive to the needs of all learners.

Moreover, the role of teachers as lifelong learners must be celebrated, as their own development is intricately tied to the success of their students. Teachers who embrace their own journeys of self-discovery and growth are better equipped to foster the same in their students. When educators continually reflect on their practices, challenge their assumptions, and seek new avenues for growth, they not only enhance their teaching but also serve as powerful role models for the students they mentor. In this way, education becomes a reciprocal relationship—a shared journey of growth, mutual respect, and understanding between students and teachers alike.

In the context of global challenges, such as climate change, technological advancements, and shifting social dynamics, education must evolve to address the needs of the future. Preparing students for the future is no longer just about imparting knowledge—it's about cultivating the skills and mindsets necessary to navigate complex problems and thrive in a rapidly changing world. Critical thinking, creativity, adaptability, and emotional intelligence are skills that need to be integrated into the curriculum to ensure students are equipped for the challenges ahead. By embedding these skills within the learning process, educators can help students become more than just knowledgeable individuals—they can become leaders, innovators, and compassionate global citizens.

In this journey, we must also acknowledge the importance of community in the learning process. Education does not take place in isolation; it thrives in a network of relationships that support and nurture growth. Schools, families, communities, and society at large must work together to create an environment where learning is a shared experience, grounded in trust, respect, and collaboration. When the broader community is involved in the educational process, students are not only supported academically but also emotionally, socially, and culturally. This holistic approach to education ensures that students are well-rounded individuals who are prepared to contribute positively to their communities and the world.

Finally, as we continue to evolve as educators and lifelong learners, we must never lose sight of the deeper purpose of education: to inspire, to challenge, and to empower individuals to reach their fullest potential. Education is not merely about the accumulation of knowledge; it is about transformation. It is about guiding individuals on a path of self-discovery, where they not only learn facts but also develop the wisdom, empathy, and courage to navigate the complexities of life. By embracing the transformative power of education, we ensure that every learner—whether teacher or student—can step into the future with hope, purpose, and the capacity to make a positive impact on the world.

Printed in Dunstable, United Kingdom